THE ELEMENTS OF DREAMWORK

Strephon Kaplan-Williams is an internationally recognised author in the field of growth psychology. He founded the first dreamwork centre, the Jungian-Senoi Institute in America and works as a therapist as well as lecturing widely on this and related subjects. Based in the UK, Strephon also trains people in what he calls Mandala Dreamwork Training indicating his emphasis on both wholeness and dreamwork generally. Strephon and his associates also trained people with *Dream Cards* a revolutionary dreamwork and life tool for personal transformation.

The *Elements Of* is a series designed to present high quality introductions to a broad range of essential subjects.

The books are commissioned specifically from experts in their fields. They provide readable and often unique views of the various topics covered, and are therefore of interest both to those who have some knowledge of the subject, as well as to those who are approaching it for the first time.

Many of these concise yet comprehensive books have practical suggestions and exercises which allow personal experience as well as theoretical understanding, and offer a valuable source of information on many important themes.

In the same series

THE ELEMENTS OF
DREAMWORK

Strephon Kaplan-Williams

ELEMENT

Shaftesbury, Dorset ● Rockport, Massachusetts
Brisbane, Queensland

© Strephon Kaplan–Williams 1990

First published in Great Britain in 1990 by
Element Books Limited
Shaftesbury, Dorset

Published in the USA in 1991 by
Element, Inc.
42 Broadway, Rockport, MA 01966

Published in Australia in 1991 by
Element Books Limited for
Jacaranda Wiley Limited
33 Park Road, Milton, Brisbane, 4064

Reprinted 1991
Reprinted 1993
Reprinted 1994

Cover illustration by Hanife Hassan O'Keeffe
Cover design by Max Fairbrother
Typeset by Selectmove Ltd, London
Printed and bound in Great Britain by
Biddles Ltd, Guildford & King's Lynn

British Library Cataloguing in Publication Data
Kaplan–Williams, Strephon
The elements of dreamwork.
1. Dreams
I. Title
154.63

Library of Congress Cataloging in Publication
Data available

ISBN 1–85230–158–9

CONTENTS

The dreams and dreamwork used in this book are from real people with their permission. Yet they are also examples of dreams that could come from more than one person, so I suggest that no one identify with any material here but simply see it as useful for illustration purposes.

To all the dreamworkers on this earth who have kindly lent of their dreams, their courage, and their dreamwork, and who are fast becoming Spiritual Warriors.

THE DREAM WARRIOR CREDO

I have no dreams, I am born in the night

I have no problems, my problems I take as my own and give them to nobody

I have no lust, I live creatively life's energies as they arise in me

I have no love, I express caring and passion in all that I do

I have no innocence, I take things openly as they come

I have no guilt, I have betrayed no one by meeting their expectations

I have no hate, all can deny me at any place and at any time

I have no anger, I am continually wounded by the rough edges of life

I have no peace, my heart is full of emptiness as I let all of life in

I have no centre, the centre is not where I can place it

I have no I, the I that is me resides in all my choices

I have no life, what I want is not what I get

I have no death, there is no place that I can call home

Strephon Kaplan-Williams

INTRODUCTION

At the time of this writing I am training around a hundred people in dreamwork who have given a year's commitment to an ongoing programme, Mandala Dreamwork Training™, under the direction also of four other dreamwork leaders. This amazing commitment to personal transformation through dreamwork signifies to me that we now have a solid and comprehensive approach which will continue to expand over the next years well into the twenty-first century.

This short book gives me the opportunity to present our key methods and principles with many examples of dreamwork from students and teachers as well as from myself. Ten years ago I published the *Jungian-Senoi Dreamwork Manual* (*The Dreamwork Manual*, British edition). It has continued to sell well as the classic reference book for in-depth dreamwork by individuals and groups. This present book adds a clarity and perspective I had not achieved then but which is central to the work now. The methodology is still there with new methods added. The examples are new. In some ways I see this book as a fundamental statement of position on the value of dreamwork as a separate profession from psychotherapy or other personal growth approaches. Yet it is not what many dreamwork teachers are doing. Our methodology is more complete, more evocative of healing and spiritual perspective. We also go beyond the methods to the actual practice in living transformed lives as we truly follow the dream and not the egocentric point of view. I would suggest the following guidelines for the work.

1. Nothing happens without a commitment and regular practice. Make a commitment to following your dreams through dreamwork and your life will change, even from the first dreamwork you do. True knowledge comes only after commitment and not before it.

2. Make your commitment to wholeness and individuation as well as to the practice of dreamwork. Dreamwork is a powerful methodology, but it is not the method which counts but the person practising it. Dreams are not to serve the ego but the ego to serve the dreams, and the Dream Source from which they originate. Dreams are more whole than we are in our conscious viewpoint. They present all sides of ourselves for integration and actualisation. Individuation means following one's own unique destiny as revealed from sources within and without other than ego. We choose Life, not the fulfilment of needs and desires.

3. Bring resolution to every conflict both inner and outer, no matter what price you pay to do it. What all dreams ask of us is to resolve the issues raised in dreams and in life. This requires integrity and giving up acting from the defence system. No matter how much you resist something, let go and follow through to the source. Your life is not your own once you have made a fundamental commitment to follow your dreams as they lead you on the journey to meaning and wholeness.

4. In weekly practice always objectify the dream in some way, then include the dream ego's relation to what is happening in the dream. Get clear on the issues and what needs resolving in the dream. Then go on to do any of the dreamwork practices. End every session with reflection upon what has happened for you. Consciousness is the result of experience. It does not precede it.

5. Never become caught in any one method, principle, or point of view. Wholeness means practising all points of view in an integrative way. There are no absolutes in this system but plenty of process. Once you have achieved a value, start at the beginning again.

6. Our fundamental commitment is to follow the dream, and each night new dreams come. We never stop dreaming, and we can commit ourselves to never stopping working with the dream, our own as well as those of others.

7. We dream to wake to life because life would put us to sleep with all its demands. We never yield the inner to the outer but combine both for living the journey towards meaning and wholeness.

THINGS TO DO

We suggest you buy a journal, a blank book, which is private to you, and which you ask no one else to look at or read. You have that right. In the journal you record your dreams and any thoughts upon waking in the morning. Do not worry about whether you remember a dream or not. Simply record your thoughts first thing when you wake up.

Now in your journal or on a piece of paper, please write responses to the following:

- Why are you reading this book? What is your need? What is your desire? One motivation is negative? One is positive?
- What is evoked for you personally so far in reading the material? Remember you can agree or differ with the author all the way through. There are no absolutes. If you find yourself evoked or inspired, write about it and get to your own questions, values, and position.

1 · THE DREAM JOURNEY

What we relate to out there reflects what we are like inside.

A woman dreamed of herself sitting contemplating a flower
slowly unfolding at its own pace.

Taking the dream journey has always made a significant difference in
people's lives. We can live at the surface or we can go deeply into our
experience to find meaning. To live at the surface is to participate in
life without any reflection, having babies, turning out productive work,
worrying about our issues, crying, laughing, going through depression,
worshipping within a religious tradition, watching television, making
a telephone call, all the many things we call life. These experiences are
real. No one can doubt them, but at the same time they often appear
re-enacted in dreams. This we call the *inner life*, as contrasted with
the *outer life*.

Would you not also like to know who you are inside yourself at the
same time you participate in the many activities of the outside world?
This is what dreamwork is about. It takes us deeper to where we can
live changed lives. Living the everyday life has its rewards, especially
when things are going well. Yet when such dramas as accident, divorce,
depression, crime, loss of job or relationship, sickness, children leaving
home, world crises, intervene then we begin to question what it's all
about and what we are doing with ourselves.

Would you really want to miss the purpose for your life? Is there a

1

purpose? Conceivably it is not enough to simply live life as we can, earn more income, develop skill in an activity, steal a kiss, make love the 5000 times life gives us, receive another kiss, adventure in safe territory.

1. WE DREAM TO WAKE TO LIFE!

What do dreams say? How does working with dreams help with our issues?

Each night we sleep and dream. We dream yet do little work with our dreams. It is as if we are given as our birthright a field full of buried treasure, and after a rain (are these our tears?) a little gold shows through. We see it, touch it even, yet we do not commit ourselves to digging for the full potential.

Modern research has discovered what the ancients always knew, that dreams are a necessary part of our mental health. That within the psyche, within the inner life of personality dynamics, there is a natural self-regulating centre which helps us process life. Each night this integrative centre, the Dream Source, is sending us messages which give the current issues of our lives and what to do about them. Yet many of us remain ignorant of our deepest selves. We do not know how to read the messages or participate actively in the dream process. An *issue* is an unresolved problem, a new potential and a choice point for change.

We take the outer journey in life yet we do not take the dream journey. We even dream and remember some of our dreams yet we do no dreamwork with them. We amass more money, create and raise children, buy a bigger house. We do not take the inward journey to find who we are as individuals with a unique purpose to fulfil.

And when death takes us, what have we? Am I the house I so lovingly painted and lived in? Am I my two children now living their lives as adults? Am I the clothes I wore, the sculptures I made, the businesses I created, the court cases I won, the books I wrote, the letters I sent, the partners I loved, the food I ate, the friends I had, the religion I worshipped in, the country I gave my allegiance to? Am I any of these when I die?

It is as if I am nothing if I have not discovered my true self as one who follows the *inner journey* and realises the meaning and fullness of his-her life. I have been only half alive if I have not developed the inner life as well as the outer life. One way to do this is to learn dreamwork as a practice, to take the dream journey, letting it lead you to places you would never go, things you would never do, ways of being you would never develop, without the dream as evoker and guide.

2. TO DEVELOP OUR PERSONALITY WE MUST BECOME SELF-REFLECTIVE.

You do not have to become a psychologist to know yourself, yet you do have to become self-reflective and self-aware. The great irony is in falling asleep, in going unconscious, we have our greatest experiences of potential wakefulness. The dreams come, doing things to our dream ego, the image of ourselves in the dream, and thus try to make us aware of who we are. Yet it is hardly possible to use dreams for self-reflection and personal development unless we do dreamwork with them.

Example: A mother of two young children dreamed she was next to her opened oven door giving birth to a baby girl. Her husband walks in behind her as she delivers the baby rather awkwardly on to the floor. She is impressed with how quickly and easily the child comes out, just as in her outer childbirth experiences. The baby looks up at her and smiles adorably. But the dreamer is worried about bleeding to death because she still has the placenta inside. Someone says to suckle the baby. That will expel the placenta and the baby loves to suck. But she is frightened by the bleeding. She gets on her brother's motorbike and drives down the hill almost too fast, going around a corner and into a clothes shop which she later remembers was called 'Bewise'.

Comment: This dreamwork training student and professional woman remembers this first dream as the one which shocked and excited her into going into therapy. It has many of the key elements of beginning the Journey. There is the birth which must happen, the *inevitable step* into the future, and the *cost* of that birth, the bleeding, the *wounding*, and the need to *release* what is inside her. The dream *frightened* her, giving *negative motivation* creating the *necessity to change*. It also encouraged her with the *ease* and *intensity* of the birth, *done by herself*, and the *lovableness* of the child. At the time the dreamer was not that happy with her life, her marriage, her sense of herself, and where she was going. She needed to make changes, to take a *solitary journey*, and to *arrive* at a place where *wisdom* and *consciousness* were *central*, the Bewise clothing shop, *the place of change*.

Since that first initial dream this woman has made changes in her life. Not only did she wake up from that dream on that fateful day, she woke up from her life and made the necessary shifts to become more whole and individual within herself. Yes, the birth, the potential is there, and it needs nurturing. First the dreamer must take care of herself, she must deal with the recognition that she will bleed to death if she does not seek help. She must take care of her own problems and then she can

3

nurture and protect the new life. Yet, as the dream indicates, if she also nurtures the new life it will help her expel that which is keeping her losing her life energy, the bleeding. The placenta of the old life is no longer useful. The next stage has arrived, whether she chooses to go with it or not. Thus do dreams show us at an amazing level the condition of our deepest being, and what we must do to actualise the next step in our lives. Choice is needed. Often it is both negative and positive motivation which challenge one to choose change. Now she is different as she has made changes and made her life more conscious through therapy and dreamwork.

She has begun the Journey. She has her search for meaning, for direction in life. Many things have come up in dreams. In working with this material she has discovered much. This dreamer has recognised her part in the process. She has not just seen her problems and opportunities as outer manifestations. She has made the fundamental realisation that what happens out there is also inside oneself. The dreams and dreamwork have been powerful emotional movers. She has also been inspired by others in her dream group as each of them share and go through emotional experiences to find more of themselves, to develop choices and perspectives in dealing with life. *Dreamwork is the application of methods for actualising dream content in the personality and in one's everyday life.*

3. THE DREAM JOURNEY REFLECTS THE UNDERLYING PATTERN IN OUR LIVES.

The Journey Archetype itself is a primary energy pattern in life. All novels seem to have journey motifs. People are going places, inner and outer. They have goals, yet where they usually end up is different from where they originally intended. Symbols for the journey include the clock, the calendar, a light ahead, roads, pathways, a mountain, a tree, a boat on the water, vehicles such as trains, planes, cars, and our own feet. The journey functions in us as the developmental process, growing up, maturing, and old age. Moving forward in life is the essence of journey energy. We move forward by developing ourselves, not by achieving goals, as so many of us are trying to do.

The great opposite to the Journey Archetype is the archetype of Death-Rebirth. An *archetype* is a fundamental energy pattern or dynamic in life and in ourselves. We see Death-Rebirth energy active in great transitions such as marriage and divorce, when one cycle completes itself and another begins, thus originating a next step or stage in life. The Journey Archetype and the Death-Rebirth

Archetype have their intersection at the *Self*, the central archetype. We celebrate this *synchronicity*, or meaningful intersection, on our birthdays. A yearly cycle has completed itself. We are a year older. The New Year is also an intersection point when cyclic, or Death-Rebirth, and linear, or Journey, time meet.

In the previous dream example we note certain primaries of the Journey Archetype. There is a journeyer in terms of the dreamer who is having various reactions to what is happening. Many dreamers come to dreamwork scared of their adversaries. They have a nightmare and wake themselves instead of staying in the dream situation. So to take a journey means a *commitment* to dealing with whatever comes up, including that which would limit or destroy you.

We can often see the nature of the dream journey by working with the earliest remembered dream of our childhood. For we seem to remember such dreams because they embody a fundamental pattern in our lives.

Example: A woman dreamed a recurrent dream that as a child she was in her father's garage while a tiger tried to get in through the door. She would block one door and the tiger would go to the other door, and she had to keep running back and forth with no way to handle the situation. (Adversarial Dream pointing out the dreamer's basic mythic life pattern.)

Comment: In her adult life she often found herself in impossible situations, like having two boyfriends at the same time, and with no way of resolving them. Guided Dream Re-entry, seeing and participating in the dream again with eyes closed, enabled the dreamer to see other alternatives, such as leaving the garage or making friends with the tiger by letting him in. She learned she always had some choice in every situation, rather than an impossible dilemma. What if she had not done dreamwork on this dream and thus found a way to change her approach to life?

4. TRUE KNOWLEDGE COMES ONLY FROM COMMITMENT.

There are certain things which we cannot know without first making a *commitment* to stay present with a situation and deal with whatever arises. A commitment is a sustained choice towards a goal or value over a definite period of time. A commitment to dreamwork means a willingness to stay in the dream to face whatever the Dream Source presents us with. Your journey will not be all sweetness and light. Your attitudes may lead you to want the light and not darkness, yet in this life

5

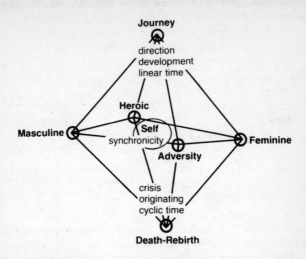

Figure 1 Seven Basic Archetypes model in which the great archetypal opposites are represented as nodes of a crystal with the most central of all, the Self, being at the centre. The Archetypes of Journey and Death-Rebirth are in relation to each other with the Central Archetype of the Self at the centre between them representing their intersection. Some of their chief dynamics of how life energy functions are represented in the diagram. For a detailed description of the model and its use with dreams see Chapter 6, The Major Dreamwork Methods.

you must have both. As in the Grail legend the ancients knew the quest was what was important and not the goal. The light which guides us can never be ours to attain and possess. It must always be just out of reach so we will go on. Thus *the journey is not what you expect but what you get.* As in dreams so in life. The unexpected is what you can expect.

Is the journey then a process or a goal, or both? So often in dreams we are presented with situations to resolve and not the resolution.

Example: Another dreamer dreamed of herself sitting contemplating a flower slowly unfolding at its own pace. She is dealing with her impatience in trying to control the unfolding. (Confirming dream strengthening the dreamworker's new attitude of being in the moment and going with life to its own rhythm.)

Comment: In her dream she finally abandons herself to the journey process embodied in the flower's unfolding at its own pace. It is beautiful and she feels good she can practise going with things rather than trying to control them. The dream confirms and reinforces the work she is doing in the dream group.

5. DREAMS SHOW US FEAR AND HOW TO COPE WITH IT.

Just as around a quarter of our dreams have sexual or feeling-relational themes, so roughly another half show us dealing with adversity and conflict. What we look for here is the ability of the person as represented by the dream ego to stay present in the dream, having feeling responses and taking action. The *dream ego* is the image of the dreamer in the dream. Another of the major archetypal configurations comes into play, that of Adversity versus the Heroic. In literature, as in life, there always seem to be characters representing the good or the bad side of life. Thus we have the major archetype of Adversity, that energy in ourselves and in life which destroys and opposes. And in conflict with this major dynamic is the Heroic Archetype, that which saves and wins victory. The Saviour and the Hero are two personifications of this archetype. The intersection between Adversity and Heroic is again the *Self*, whose chief archetypal characteristics here are *struggle* and *conflict*. In dreamwork we look to how the dream ego relates to these energies, and even embodies them. This shows up clearly in this dream from a highly creative man in his late thirties.

Examples: The dreamer is in an enclosed basement of a house and he enters the inner room. There he sees with terror and awe a large white-shaped, bird-like figure which has no eyes. The bird starts coming towards him and he decides to let it out rather than board it back up. Outside it becomes a giant black bird which flies low around the pasture and woods. The dreamer is apprehensive yet does not panic. (Adversarial dream in which the dreamer is challenged to give up control and relate. Also a Revelatory dream which gives the dreamer a major life task in changing his attitudes and behaviour.)

Comment: The dreamer had just moved from England to California and was dealing with finding a place to live and otherwise settle in, including beginning his first marriage. He had left his country to join our dreamwork training programme, and now he was being confronted through dreams and life with major adversarial forces. As he was a man there were many dreams of violence and fear, reflecting perhaps the collective male's training of coping through aggressive behaviour. Here his dream ego does not keep the scary thing in but lets it out where it takes on its natural character. The dreamer feels fear and awe. He has been given enormous things to deal with. We recalled with him other Adversarial dreams with which he had completed dreamwork. For this dream his dream ego action was dynamic already. He chose to paint the dream scene, as well as apply its teaching to his life. *Release that which you fear and you will no longer fear it. Cage what you fear and it will terrorise you forever.* We may be sure he confronted some new things with his new wife after this dreamwork!

6. JOURNEY MOTIFS IN DREAMS MAY SHOW US HOW WE MOVE THROUGH LIFE.

Example: A woman dreamed she was on a hospital trolley pushing herself along down the middle of the street. (Revelatory Dream revealing the way the dreamer moves through life.)

Comment: She did not know what her dream meant and thought because a trolley is used for wheeling you into surgery, it had something to do with illness, though she was not sick at the time. Instead of interpreting the dream for her, we did Symbol Immersion, a powerful dreamwork process technique in which you close your eyes and visualise your dream symbol as close to as it was in your original dream. (See Chapter 6, The Major Dreamwork Methods.)

The Symbol Immersion: The dreamer was asked to close her eyes and simply see the trolley again and herself on it. At first she was recalling the original dream as it was, telling it in the past tense. Now she was asked to simply experience directly a part of her dream, the symbol of herself on the trolley. This time she was again going down the main street pushing herself on the trolley. She encountered no obstacles or traffic lights. And no one thought she looked odd. She came out of her brief experience and was asked how it felt, and how it might contrast with her outer life? She liked the ease and freedom she felt in the Symbol Immersion and said her outer life was anything but easy. So her outer life dream task was to then see if there were ways she could journey in outer life with the ease and freedom she experienced on her trolley.

Comment: This second dream example again illustrates the journey motif yet at a more everyday level. What is important is the dreamer was given a new way to approach her daily life. Perhaps she did have certain attitudes which saw life as more difficult than it was? Perhaps she needed to let go more with the flow of life instead of determining it? When you are on that trolley in the hospital you have made a choice to give over control to the medical personnel as they operate on you. In the dream we see the paradox. She is both the one being pushed, or 'going with,' and the one pushing, the directing part of herself. *We have to go through life, one way or another, so it is better to develop a conscious style in how we journey.*

7. DREAMS CAN SHOW THE SYMBOLIC NATURE OF WHAT WE EXPERIENCE.

Example: A woman hurt her knee, and the night before she was to go to the hospital for a medical test and possible operation she had a dream. In the dream she is in the hospital. They put a catheter in her leg vein and give her a narcotic through it. She does not like losing her awareness and goes to the bathroom where she pees out the effects. She comes back and sits on the gurney, ready for the test. (Prospective dream indicating physical self-healing is possible if she changes her attitude and actions. Not a compensatory to conscious attitude dream since here the dream shows a prospect, a way out.)

Comment: When she woke with this dream her knee felt almost fully recovered, and she cancelled the test and the operation. From the dream she realised she could handle her symptoms herself and did not need to be dependent on the doctors. She treated her affliction as symbolic, took action herself, and the affliction was alleviated through self-healing. She did not have the problem again.

Often physical symptoms symbolise other dynamics active within ourselves. If we can get to them our symptoms can be healed. It is as if the body itself is a dream which when we understand and work with it, becomes balanced and integrated once again. Thus the dream guided this dreamer to experience her symptom, the hurt knee, as symbolic rather than literal. Had she continued in the medical model with its literal point of view who knows what would have happened? How many millions of hysterectomies have been performed because bleeding symptoms were seen as physically caused instead of symbolic expression?

Caution: Consciousness must be applied in both directions. We need to make our wounds conscious and deal with them symbolically. Yet we also need to make realistic decisions about physical symptoms when these persist or intensify having been worked with symbolically. The important thing is not to have a bias towards the physical over the symbolic, or the symbolic over the physical, but to include both.

Dreams seem more to explore issues than give answers. They open the door to process. They do not determine it.

Working spiritually we can never know whether one thing causes another. We work with the dreams and other dynamics to see what is occurring symbolically so the person can make changes in the inner as well as outer life. *Dreams will present life issues and our need to change ourselves long before physical illness challenges us to change emotionally*, when it may be too late physically to heal except from the surgeon's knife, if ever that works spiritually.

One woman got breast cancer and could not understand why, after she had finally made the choice for new life in leaving her oppressive husband, she should be so afflicted. Another woman in middle age loved her perfect breasts, seeing them as those of a young woman, and hers were removed by the surgeon because of cancer. Yet another came to see me with a dream telling her she should have changed three years ago. Now she has cancer. The list is endless of those who severely hesitate before the march of time.

Life transitions can be dangerous. Make your changes in attitude and action when the moment is right and you may not have to have life forcing a transition on you through accident or illness. Dreams will give you your issues in time yet you need a commitment to following dreams and working through to their messages.

8. DREAMS CAN SYMBOLISE NEW POTENTIAL TO REALISE IN OURSELVES AND LIFE.

Example: After a period of intense inner activity a dreamer in the dream group dreamed she was in her favourite library to do more reading. She picked a book off the shelf and in it were pictures of beautiful couples. On the next page were the words, 'The world is waiting.' (Revelatory dream indicating the moment was right and necessary to change her behaviour.)

Comment: This dream marked a dramatic transition point in this person's life. She recognised it was time to strongly involve herself in the world again. Her general attitude was *books were more interesting than people*. How many readers have this attitude? Yet, unlike books, people are more changeable and interactive. She made several outer related choices, and took her dream as a statement she is ready to make a shift in her life.

We see from this something about the nature of the dream journey. The natural predisposition of this dreamer was towards books and the realm of the imagination. This is her ego point of view. Yet she was also unhappy and unfulfilled in certain major ways. So the dream, as well as others of her dreams, came to tell her ego, her choicemaker, it is time to change focus. It does not indicate what to do but offers direction. 'The world is waiting.' What would you do if you received such a dream? People have literally changed their lives based on inner direction being revealed to them.

SUMMARY

These comments and examples are the first steps in taking a dream journey by reading and working with this book. We shall make many statements about life and about the dream journey. We shall also give many dream and life examples which come from active dreamers committed to their own dreamwork as a tool for direction and transformation in their lives.

THINGS TO DO

This is our second practice session. These suggestions for writing responses come out of the material you have just read.

- How do you interpret dreams or people's behaviour? Practise instead giving your own reactions. Not, 'I think your dream means . . . ' but 'Your dream evokes for me . . . ', and then you tell about your feelings and experience.

- Always try to turn insight into question. Not, 'I think you should do such and such.' but, 'What would it be like if you tried such and such?' Or, 'This is what I think of. What do you think of?'

- Write freely without thinking to the question, 'What is the purpose of my life now?' Evaluate. Have you written mainly about the outer life of people and things, or also about the inner life of values, choices, and meaning?

- What are you doing these days to increase your consciousness about yourself and life? Write about this, please.

- Write a one-page description of yourself. Later you may be asked to compare this with a description of yourself as you appear and act in your dreams.

- This is an advanced question, but what is the underlying pattern of your life so far? And how has it manifested in life and in dreams? This will take you at least a week to go into!

- What commitments are you making in your life at present and what are the results?

- Look closely at your way of travel in a dream. Then see in what

11

ways that applies to how you journey in your outer life, even if it is simply getting the keys and driving to the shops. There is insight here on how you live the life journey.

- If you are being stirred up about some outer life situation, try writing it up in your journal as a dream. Remember nothing is real out there, it just appears so. What may be happening is the playing out of what is inner turmoil and creativity. *What we relate to out there reflects what we are like inside.*

- If you are sick or having physical symptoms, describe them as a dream. The body is a great dream, an energy system. Draw your body and label the parts symbolically and what is happening to them. Then draw your centre and how it can act to have all the parts of yourself interrelating with each other.

- Look through your dreams until you find one that represents new potential in living life. Then devise a life task, a specific action you will take to bring some of that potential into life itself.

2 · THE BASICS OF DREAMWORK

The universal language of the unconscious is imagery.

A thirty-nine-year-old woman dreamed she was given an amber-coloured crystal and held it to her heart, creating in her an intense energy sensation.

At this time in the last decade of the twentieth century, the end of a millennium actually, we may well be at the birth of a major cultural and spiritual epoch. It has been said people are more inwardly searching when a period of 1000 years is ending. And so it is. We have in the last seventy-five years been through devastating world wars, and have now created for ourselves, or a small minority have created for us, the incredible nuclear power to destroy all of humankind within a few weeks. This nuclear umbrella means it would be mass suicide for nation to fight nation. This may happen. Picture in your mind's eye the worst possible nightmare you or anyone could have and that would be nuclear war, the fantasy made real in outer reality. We are still facing the wrong end of the trigger with the maniacs of political power squinting down the sight at us if we make one false move.

Yet on the positive side, all of us living today are at the most crucial evolutionary stage in all history. This is *the evolutionary stage of collective as well as individual individuation and wholeness.* Already there are people dealing with their problems and integrating their psyches consciously in ways which are not a threat to others. This can happen for the whole world as mass communications continue to develop, spreading the messages of hope, reconciliation and conscious integration.

Some day soon sufficient enlightenment may come to the world's cultures and they will make the telephone and transportation systems free to all users so we can relate to each other as one humanity. Such a move would cost a small part of what military armaments cost today, and would do more to prevent war than almost anything. Yet technological communication is the outward form of inner communication. One major practice which needs to be imparted to all peoples within the next 100 years is inner awareness via integrating projections.

A *projection* is the seeing as out there what is inside. World wars have always been perpetuated by using propaganda to evoke the shadow projection among the young, the least integrated. Each of us has a *shadow* side, a repressed side of what we have rejected about ourselves. This comes up in dreams when there are characters we do not like who invade our space, and when we behave in ways we would not in our public and outer life.

Some of us see dreamwork as a major contribution and practice which can also be done around the world. There may soon be data banks of symbolism and techniques for people to do from their computers, and thus work on their dreams, and projections, at home while at the same time having access to the world's knowledge about the inner life. Dreamwork needs to become a curriculum course in schools starting in the early grades. We need to realise again what past peoples recognised, the value of working with dreams for an enormous and world-wide increase in creativity and personal growth. The methodology for productive and transformative dreamwork is available now. The results are good. Will the educators see this and reconstruct their curriculums for the new evolutionary thrust, rather than keep to studying the past or enhancing business practices only? Those who do not let go of the past are condemned to repeat it. The true technological advances will always be of the human spirit and mind, and not of the machine. This is what evolution is all about. *Machines are manifestations of the mind, not mind of the machine.*

There are still several blocks to a new age of vitality where the inner life is given its due as a source of transformation in dealing with the outer life. *We need an ecology not only of the environment but also of the heart.*

This same conflict of the old way of rational exploitation of world resources without regard for heart values comes up in the dreamwork movement. For the big struggle is between the rationalists, the interpreters, and those who would do dreamwork process. There are several things wrong with the interpretive model, and these must be made as clear as possible so we each have a choice as to how we will work with our dreams. To understand these issues we must go through the basics.

9. THE WHOLE OF LIFE, THE PSYCHE, THE UNIVERSE ITSELF, RESTS ON AN ARCHETYPAL BASE.

An *archetype* is a basic energy cluster made up of energy and form. *Energy* is the ability to move, to go from one place to another. It has force, a degree of power, the ability to affect or produce changes in matter. *Matter* is itself a more solid state of energy. Matter is the form energy takes when it is at relative rest. The archetype is defined as energy and form combined together. Energy without form would be diffuse. Form without energy would be without movement, and in human terms, without life. The universe is made up of these basic clusters of energy and form called archetypes. Life itself is a manifestation of these basic units.

Dreamwork works with archetypal energy in the dream, in the psyche, and in life. We experience in dreams the patterns of how life energy is blocked or is expressing itself. *All energy is either in resistance or release*. We work with dreams to free our energy so it may function naturally and integratively. Since dreams reveal how the life energy is moving or blocked, dreamwork is one of the best approaches for working with the life energy for healing and fulfilment.

All archetypes and their manifestations exist within a *wholeness pattern* residing in life itself and in the psyche. Each archetype is related to each of the other archetypes based on universal and natural laws. These are the laws of opposition and reconciliation with their various forms of expression and functioning reduced to specific dynamics, the *principles* by which we choose to live, and the *functions*, the natural ways of expressing live energy.

We look to our dreams to see how we are, or are not, expressing life energy, and then apply methods to evoke the natural wholeness pattern, often moving through blocks, to new life expression and vitality.

The Seven Basic Archetypes Model

The Seven Basic Archetypes Model used here helps the reader see how energy works in life, in dreams, and in the psyche. It also has applications to history and culture, as in figure 2.

To state the introduction to this chapter in archetypal terms, the world today needs unity, a function of the central archetype of the *Self*, or it will destroy itself. We have the potential today, residing in the archetype of *Adversity*, to utterly annihilate all but the most rudimentary forms of life on this planet. These nuclear missiles were built by an over *masculinised* consciousness that saw power and domination as the way to protect nations instead of using *feminine* values of creativity and relatedness to bind nations together. Conflicts will always be present. There must be struggle and separation between positive and negative. But each side sees itself as the good, the *Heroic*, and the other side as the bad, the *Adversary*, the enemy.

The way to handle conflict is to see these perceptions as projections of archetypal forces from within ourselves. We each have all the archetypes within us, which come out in our dreams. If there is inner violence then the enemy is also within. We are the enemy as well as the reconciler and saviour. We have all these parts within us but they need to work within a cooperative wholeness pattern. This means we make the dynamics conscious by withdrawing projections and integrating them within ourselves. Each step of life, the *Journey*, takes us onward. We evolve, we become more conscious as well as more effective. But there are also challenges on the way, the *Death-Rebirths*, which demand radical change from us. Every crisis is an opportunity for change. Shall we choose the whole process? For this we need a creative and committed *ego* or choicemaker which sees the total and serves the *Self*, the centre within and without, whose functions are to unify, to differentiate, to integrate all opposites into one whole for the transformed life.

Dreams and other methods of knowing will show us the way. For they point to the inner dynamics motivating outer behaviour. We start at home, and return home at every juncture and crisis, to ask once again, how am I being affected by what is outside me and what can I do to make things more conscious and integrated? We each have that choice, both as nations and as individuals.

10. A DREAM IS ENERGY IN IMAGERY FROM A SOURCE OTHER THAN EGO.

What we call dreams are not dreams, but *dream reports*. The original dream may be an experience of energy which our minds turn into images to more easily grasp and remember these states. The mind might also translate these images finally into concepts.

16

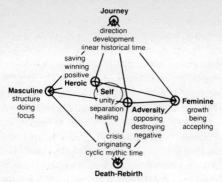

Figure 2   The Seven Basic Archetypes Unified Field Model of how energy works in the psyche and in outer life.

Thus the original dream experience is likely to be a shifting and transforming energy pattern, which then is translated into images and actions. The shifts in energy patterns are perceived first through the mind's image-making function, then these images are in turn perceived and logically processed as concepts.

Example. The author woke up on Good Friday and had a dream of a complete prayer being given him. The most primary experience he could recall was an intense energy state. Still in this state he immediately wrote out the dream prayer exactly as it came to him. There was no conscious construction involved. He simply listened, immersed in the energy, and wrote what came. The prayer turned out to be complete and meaningful in itself. He had begun with energy and moved to concept. Thus he knew he dreamed the prayer, and wrote it, yet what he first woke with was an intense feeling state, quickly followed by the prayer. (Great dream experienced as a direct transmission of meaning from the centre.)

11. DREAMS ARE PRODUCED BY THE INTEGRATIVE CENTRE IN THE PSYCHE.

The following is a model of how the psyche works in centring us and producing dreams. Have a look first at the *ego*. When we fall asleep we let go of *volitional consciousness*, the ability to direct awareness and make choices, but we do not necessarily let go of *aware consciousness*, simply being present to what is happening. So we see the *sleeping ego circle* intersecting with the *dream circle*, which in turn has been created through use of the *image-making function* by the *Self centre*

17

which has focused on two facets of the larger *psyche*, the interrelated pattern of inner dynamics. These dynamics include *patterns* in the psyche as well as *telepathic* perceptors or receptors which seem to tune into what is going on around us even while we sleep, and the whole of the psyche is stimulated by input from external events through the perceptual faculties of the physical and mental body. The Self centre is all the time actively regulating and balancing life energy in us, and maybe even in outer life. But it cannot do the whole job alone and so presents issues and potentials as 'training sessions' for the *ego function* which carries consciousness of itself, the psyche, and life, and makes crucial choices in the outer which affect the inner life as well. The Self centre thus wants to influence and train the ego through dreams, but often the ego resists this process, being afraid that letting go of what little control it has to the Self will somehow doom it to extinction. This is merely a fear on the ego's part based on traumatic experiences of the adversarial aspects of existence. The Self centre wants the ego as an ally, not an enemy, because it needs the ego function to serve the Self in its process of ongoing integration and transformation. The key stages are as follows.

Stage 1 – The centre balances energy patterns within.

The *Self, the balancing, centralising function within*, operates as the energy centre and pattern-maker in the psyche. We can feel the effects of this in different energy states, as when we feel nauseous from being psychically unbalanced or overworked. The nausea acts as a self-regulating balancing mechanism to get the organism, ourselves, to change its behaviour. The Self is always manifesting in shifting energy patterns within the scope of its functions. People can even become nauseous while working with dreams as the Self seeks to have repressed energy expressed and integrated. Sometimes dreamworkers even throw up or go into great agony. This is natural when releasing long pent-up feelings and emotions.

Stage 2 – The centre within uses the image-making function to convey the patterns we call dreams.

Perception of inner states is achieved through felt bodily responses and through imagery experiences. The Self then uses the *image-making function* of the psyche to portray energy experiences while asleep which we call dreams. It is important to make a distinction between the image-making function and the Self. For the ego, and not just the Self, can use the image-making function, as when

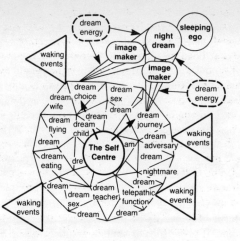

Figure 3 The psyche produces dreams in order to train the ego in serving, rather than resisting, the healing transformative process from the Self.

doing visualisation or creating imaginary scenes. The image-making function is a distinct function in the psyche which produces a language of feeling-tones images taken from the world around us, yet with an archetypal or universal transcendent base.

Stage 3 – The ego remembers the patterns as images and concepts.

The *ego function*, the conscious personality which makes choices and focuses energy and awareness, then remembers these images and energy states and begins translating them into concepts for easier comprehension and recall.

Example: This is a dream many people have had. The dreamer dreamed she had a dream and woke herself up. However, she found she was still in her dream. She was dreaming she woke up! She then turned on the light to make sure she was awake. She seemed awake but then found she was not awake. Finally she gave up in frustration trying to wake up to write her dream, and wrote it down in the morning. (Consciousness dream showing the nature of the dreamer's consciousness.)

Comment: We see the ego function at work in this dream. The dream ego thinks it is awake, thinks it is *conscious*. At the same time it experiencing *images*, the images of the bedroom, it is experiencing *concepts*, ideas about its state of consciousness. The dream ego also thinks it has made a *choice* to leave the dream state and be awake. Yet it has not made that choice but only experiences choice as imagery and thought, and not action. Finally, based on a feeling of frustration, the dream ego gives up determining or controlling the action. We have imagery, feeling, and thought in this dream experience, yet what is missing is *controlling action*, an actual choice being made to open one's eyes and move from the bed.

12. LIFE PRINCIPLES MAY COME TO US AS STATEMENTS IN IMAGERY.

Sometimes our dreams give us life principles to live by. These may be in the form of concepts or imagery. Let us remind ourselves of two fundamental principles or statements: *the universal language of the unconscious is imagery*, and *Dream Actualisation means turning image into function, not concept.*

While *principles* seem to be conceptual they are descriptions of *functions*, or how energy works in the psyche and in life. Normally life principles come to us in conceptual form, such as the following heard in the author's dream, *we must not consider our healing dreams nightmares.*

Now compare the above with this principle in imagery from a woman's dream: *you have to put a white dress into muck to have it come out cleaner.*

Example: The original dream reported was, I had this white dress with dots and a large collar and for some reason I had to put it into this pail of disgusting muck. When I pulled it out it was completely white. I was surprised, because it didn't make sense to me.

Comment: Here we have a teaching story in the form of a dream. The dreamer was asked to resay the dream as a 'principle in imagery,' and then to say it conceptually. Her rational mind told her it did not make sense. If you plunged a white dress into muck it would come out dirty. Cause and effect. With symbols we enter the world of *paradox*, where things are not either-or, but both. We did not attempt to interpret the dream for the dreamer. The suggested task was to keep this 'principle in imagery' in her mind all week and apply it to life. The principle she tried out might be stated thus,

True clarity comes out of entering the dark side and experiencing it.

To clean something we must dirty it first. Living out of an ideal is pure. Meditating is pure. Going out and getting a job is impure. Bringing the ideal into reality dirties it with compromise, experience, and change. *Reality is where we go from potential to actual.* In dreamwork we bring the potential inherent in the symbol into life. This grounds the symbolic experience in the everyday concrete world. Our dreamer became more realistic with her life through a change of attitude. The living images of her dream are what hit home to her at a feeling level as she went out to change her life, feeling if the new focus had come in a dream it must be right for her.

13. DREAM INTERPRETATION CREATES MORE FALLACIES THAN IT CORRECTS.

Most people, and several schools of psychology, interpret dreams and believe their interpretations are real and make sense. While anyone can hit the jackpot if they pull the lever long enough on the gambling machine, the hit and miss character of dream interpretation does not justify its use. This is a challenging statement, for it cuts right into the heart of those psychologies, including the Freudian and Jungian, which based their therapy method on interpreting dreams. These psychoanalysts and analysts spend years studying cases, the works of their master, and mythology, in an attempt to back up their authority to interpret someone else's dreams for them. And they charge expensive rates for this dubious service. (No, don't put this book down now, stay with it.) The new way for psychologists and therapists of any school is to come out from behind the desk and enter into a direct therapeutic and dreamwork process with their clients. Both will be enormously changed in the process, for they will not be able to operate on the basis of intellect alone. They will have to come into their feelings in direct involvement with their clients. If they process well enough, therapists will also have healing experiences in doing dreamwork with others as well as with themselves. From having trained many therapists in this process I have found they are almost totally extended out into their clients. Their projections are enormous and the resistance great when I challenge them to integrate. I also encourage honest feedback about my projections, as well as work with them at an inner level.

We have also those psychics and other esoterics who hand out dream and life interpretations to their clients instead of entering into an active healing process with them. The world is full of the rational mind, mostly it seems to be used to support the ego's defence system. Process bypasses the defensive ego and brings out the real self.

A fundamental premise of dream interpretation is that the *symbolic images and actions of dreams mean something conceptually to a person*. The second is that *dreams speak to one about oneself and life*, the dream reflects people's psychology back to them. This is only an assumption, not a proven 'scientific' fact. Perhaps there is ultimately no proof dreams are anything more than visual energy experiences in themselves. However, we in the Jungian-Senoi approach do have the weight of hundreds of people's testimonies that working with their dreams has given them new insights and actions about themselves and life.

Dream interpreters conceptualise what the dream's images and actions mean. To interpret an image you must apply a symbol system to it. A symbol system is a body of belief which sets up a one-to-one correspondence between an image and a concept. In their belief *image equals concept*. All dream symbol books are examples of symbol systems. Images may suggest a series of concepts, yet surely there cannot be one and only one concept or interpretation for a symbol or image?

Fallacy: Making the assumption anyone can know what a symbol or image means. Perhaps image does equal concept? Yet who can prove this one-to-one correspondence between image and concept?

Example: A young psychic responded with an elaborate interpretation of the person's dream symbols to someone's sharing a dream in a dream group, 'The suitcase you are carrying in the dream is full of all the things you should get rid of in your life. You are on the promenade in your dream to enjoy yourself. But you must first get rid of what is in that suitcase weighing you down.'

Good point: Interpreting a symbol, such as in the above example, may give the dreamer new possibilities for looking at the dream if he or she is strong enough to decide which interpretations make sense and which don't. Because an interpretation sounds good does not mean it is the right one for you. Be careful. *If you choose not to believe someone else you can believe yourself.*

Errors created by the interpretive approach:

- Not following the principle of actualisation by not helping the dreamer to experience directly what might be in the dream suitcase.
- Stealing from the dreamer a feeling experience of self-discovery by giving the dreamer a concept which seems to make sense,

yet which comes from the outside. Insights from outside tend to weaken people and make them more dependent beings.

The better way:

- Ask questions of the dreamer which will create a fuller experience of the suitcase, such as the following: What does the suitcase feel like in your dream? What do you see yourself doing with the suitcase in the dream? Ask open-ended questions, questions not requiring a Yes-No or one pat answer.

- Do a Dream Re-entry in which the dreamer in the meditative state with eyes closed re-experiences the whole dream scene, including carrying the suitcase.

- Do a Symbol Immersion. If the dreamer chooses, he or she can go into the meditative state and focus on the dream suitcase again and then do something with it, perhaps even open it.

We simply do not know from the outside or from the ego's point of view what is in that suitcase if anything. In Dream Re-entry and Symbol Immersion we return to the mental state which produced the dream in the first place to experience it and its potentials more fully. Yes, the dream is still alive after being originally dreamed, even if we are not remembering it at the moment. These techniques have helped people to have profound dream and feeling experiences through accessing a dream again while in the meditative state.

What we do not do

We do not refer to categories of symbols for an interpretation, as you might with your typical symbol books in which the writers list a symbol and then say what it means, or as with the psychologies and their authoritative viewpoints.

Example: The suitcase means you have hidden stuff you are carrying around with you. Suitcase means you have hidden desires sexually since a suitcase represents the female vagina, as do the purses which women carry. Or a suitcase means you have a desire to travel.

Any of these interpretations might have some relevance, yet they tend to be seductive. The ego, or conscious side of ourselves, can be taken over by other people's thoughts. Interpretations are based on categories, or symbol systems, which represent generalities. In dreamwork our goal is to make the response to the dream specific to *the dreamer.* To do this we must evoke the dreamer's own experience. Not give him or her *outside interpretations.*

Dreamwork counterbalances projecting on to dreams.

Projection can happen when someone tries to interpret a dream symbol for someone. We put on the other person's dream image or action our own inner content.

Example: A woman shared a dream with a male friend in which they were making love. The friend suggested the dream was saying they should indeed make love. He was projecting his desire to be sexually close with the woman. She might even have wanted to be close with him sexually, yet it was her dream, a dream which would naturally evoke a projection from the male. Also, the dreamer could see her dream as an experience of inner unity between herself and the masculine side of herself. Yet even here things can become complicated. We can project our thoughts and feelings onto our dreams. She can project her longing into her dream. (Compensatory dream, most likely, presenting aspects of herself projected onto the male and therefore opposite to what she consciously identifies with in herself.)

Comment: To counterbalance projecting into this dream we might ask the dreamer to do a Dream Dialogue first with the man as an inner figure. Ask him as symbol, what do you represent to me in my dream?, and write quickly anything which comes into your head. New insight might occur. Then you have a choice whether to take the dream to the outer or not, or to discuss feelings about a possible relationship.

The fallacy of the aha!

There is a theory among current dream specialists which says the dreamer is the only interpreter of his or her dream. Thus when they feel a certain interpretation is the right one they have an 'Aha!' or 'just so' experience. This is taken as always authentic. Yet dreamers may project onto their dreams, thus missing what the dream seems to be challenging them about. We also have a theory that the dreamer is the last person to understand his or her dream since dreams compensate or show the opposite to the conscious viewpoint. C. G. Jung was of this school. Sometimes an 'aha' experience can be genuine recognition of new insight about the dream. Jeremy Taylor in his books supports this view.

Solution: To get to the meaning of your dreams do dreamwork with them using *Actualisation* techniques which make dream potentials actual by choosing to directly experience them on a feeling and outer concrete level. Rather than projecting on to the dream, do a dialogue with the dream figure and ask why are they making love together, or whatever they are doing?

Example: A woman dreamed that an aeroplane crashed. She then read in the newspaper two days later than an airliner had indeed crashed, killing everybody on board. She projected herself into her dream and assumed she had psychic ability to foretell outer events. She even wondered whether if because she dreamed the event she was in some way causing it. This belief originates from the age-old attitude that if our inner world is chaotic in a certain direction the outer world will go the same way. Thus we may project our fears and feelings both on to our dreams and on to outer life events. Yes, the inner state may indeed influence outer events, but projection is far more common and debilitating.

There will be times also when we genuinely perceive through the dream state outer events as they are happening or will happen. The fact that this psychic level seems to exist does not substitute for the amount of automatic projecting people do on to their dreams and on to their lives.

Example: A dreamer dreamed her pregnant room-mate found her boyfriend 3000 miles away, and on the same day she did find him. (Psychic or Predictive dream confirmed by journal entries based on timely reports between participants.)

Comment: Was this coincidence or was there a psychic perception involved? There are so many reports of this kind of experience we must assume some of these are valid as communication experiences rather than projections. Some commentators suggest time and space are relative to our perception of them. Thus dream perception can perceive past, present and future as happening in one simultaneous whole, and with no spatial separation between events, time being defined as the movement from one space to another.

14. DREAMWORK IS WORKING WITH A DREAM TO OBTAIN ITS MEANING.

Dreamwork contrasts with *dream interpretation* in that with dreamwork you actualise or live your dream in some way. In *dream interpretation* you rationalise what your dream means intellectually by turning image into concept.

Dream interpretation is turning image into concept using outside symbol systems. This is always suspect because firstly an image is not a concept, and secondly whether an image equals a certain concept or not is a purely arbitrary affair. (See the method, Symbol Amplification for how to relate analytically to symbols for their meaning.) *Turning image into function,* on the other hand, means trying out and living the potential which the image seems to symbolise. If we actualise the potential of a dream symbol we are activating a function within us. A *function* is the ability to act. (See Dream Actualisation method overleaf.)

Fallacy: Interpreting dreams keeps the ego in control because the ego can always build a rational picture to explain anything and keep it safe.

Corrective: Do dreamwork to actualise the potential of the dream. New ways of living will come.

Dreamwork turns image into function.

Example: A thirty-nine-year-old woman dreamed she was given an amber coloured crystal and held it to her heart, creating in her an intense energy sensation. The next day she visited a store and saw an amber crystal ball which she bought to use in her meditation. While the exact shape of the crystal was different from the dream crystal, she realised using such a crystal in meditation gave her an increased sense of being in tune with the spiritual dimension of her life. Note that you do not have to speculate about whether some sort of spiritual energy resides in a crystal or not, or whether the Self as centre is projected on to it because both are based on invisible lines of force and relation, all united in a single whole. We simply note that crystal meditation has practical value as an *evoker* of feeling and meaning.

15. ACTUALISING DREAMS BRINGS POTENTIAL INTO ACTUAL.

We *actualise* dreams by doing dreamwork with them. Instead of interpreting symbols, as in dream interpretation, we help our original dream to come alive in some new way.

Example: An older, widowed woman had not had an intimate relationship with a man since her husband had died five years earlier. In a series of dreams her relating to dream men became more and more intimate and less scary to her. She was encountering them as in life with only brief conversations and hugs, yet gradually she dreamed of being sexual with a man. In her outer life she was terribly afraid of 'interactions with the male' as she called it. But based on her work in overcoming fear and what her dreams were showing her she started going to square dances and meeting men who were sexually interested in her. (Compensatory dream moving to Teaching dreams because the dream relating is more full than the outer relating, as if leading her in little steps forward in life. Also a Confirming dream confirming previous risks taken.)

The principle here is, *Follow your dreams by doing in outer life what you are doing in your dreams.* Many people seem to act more creatively and less afraid in their dreams than they do in outer life. Dreamwork can mean living as fully in your outer life as you do in your dreams. The way to do this is to act in safe and creative ways on the potential showing in your dreams.

Example: A woman with a severely dominating husband had the following dream. She dreamed she went shopping and bought herself beautiful clothes using her bank account. She also needed more money and so wrote a large cheque on her husband's account. She bought him an expensive cake with part of his money. She awoke with a good feeling about spending her money freely on her needs and values. In terms of her actual outer life she had her own bank account yet was still quite cautious as to how she spent money, as well as keeping certain things hidden from her husband. She had not developed yet the degree of independence from him she experienced in her dreams. She also had other dreams in which she was appreciated by a considerate and sensitive lover. Interestingly enough, in the present dream she does things for herself rather than getting help and affirmation from the outside. (Compensatory dream in that the dream behaviour is much greater than the outer behaviour, showing both her inadequacy and her potential.)

Caution: Dream Actualisation does not mean literally acting out your dreams. You do not try to fly off a cliff because you fly in a dream. You do not have sex with your neighbour's partner because you are having sex with him in your dream. You recognise your sexual and intimacy feelings and translate them into appropriate and possible behaviour.

Fallacy: Using your dreams to make outer life decisions. Some people will let their dreams tell them what to do. If a dream seems to say to not marry or to marry they may try to give over their power of choice to the dream and follow it literally. More than one dream author has recommended you follow your dreams in this way. This can be dangerous and misleading to yourself and others. You make your choices based on your reasoning and feeling. Dreams are symbolic, not often literal. And dreams will sometimes give contradictory positions when an issue is followed in a series of dreams.

The Dream Actualisation approach sees dreams as representing potentials for living, not recommended choices or certainties from some divine authority represented by the dream, or the interpreter of the dream.

16. DREAMS ARE SITUATIONS AND PATTERNS NEEDING RESOLUTION.

The startling fact is most dreams are unresolved. We begin a journey, we come to a closed door, we give birth to a baby yet where is the baby, our brothers criticise us yet where is our reaction, and so on. From this clinical observation we make the following premise:

The chief function of dreaming is to create the necessity to bring resolution to blocked patterns and life issues by the ego's evoking the integrative self.

The chief function of dreaming is also to inspire the passionate commitment to developing new personality and life potential.

Dreams also function to help resolve personal and creative problems we are concerned with.

Note that dreams do not provide answers. *Dreams are questions inviting responses, not answers giving certainty.* We do the work. The Dream Source presents the difficulty and the potential. This is Dream Actualisation rather than interpretation. We do not want to know what the dream means. We passionately desire to resolve and to heal the issues it presents, and to follow new inspiration from the deep centre imaged in dreams. This is a dream of a twenty-four-year-old man, both ex-football player and possible candidate for the priesthood, although of individual mystical temperament beyond his young age which may prevent this.

Example: The man dreamed he was in his brother's truck being criticised by his older brother who kept attacking him. He held his temper as long as he could and then woke up. (Issue dream which clearly presents an inner-outer problem but without a resolution, leaving it to dreamwork to provide.)

Comment: The dreamer said this dream re-enacted a major scene when he had left his family a year ago. One of his brothers had just got married and given him the keys to take care of his truck. The rest of the family jumped on him, teasing him, trying to undermine his self-identity. He was unhappy no one had stood up for him. He kept the keys but was quite upset. As a teenager he had been so mad at his alcoholic dad he had almost killed him. The dreamer was a husky man who would naturally be afraid of his strength.

The dreamwork: The young man wanted to work on expressing the anger in the dream which he had never expressed to anyone. I as the dream group leader instructed him to lie on his back, a vulnerable position, and to hold a small pillow which he could squeeze when he felt his emotions rising. He saw again the dream and the scene and started expressing what he was unable to say before to his brother. His tears and his anger increased as I pressed certain sensitive bodywork points on his large chest. Finally he exploded and said he wanted to scream, which he did into a large pillow I handed him. More of this work led to a new sense of relaxation and knowledge of his issues. He wanted to encounter me by pushing hands, which we engaged in. Then I asked to carry all 190 lbs of him which I did for several minutes and the young man let go to his emotions and called me Dad. The transformation was almost over. The process is to get into the wound behind the repressed anger, which means expressing and going through the anger until some sense of resolution occurs. Such emotional work felt right to everyone in the room. We had shared as men. There were no women in this dream group that night.

Many workers in the healing professions might be too afraid to take an angry young man through a healing process like this. I certainly was at the personal ego level. But he was already committed and working in this ongoing dream group. What is there to lose? If we do not work with all people who demonstrate commitment in working with their dreams, then a void sucking away our integrity will begin to dominate our process. There must be a creative solution to every problem, and together we found it. Resolution here is the releasing of repressed feelings created from the family experience and presented to us by the dream to get resolved. We resolved the dream and life issue by going into the dream situation and enacting it emotionally. This releases the pent-up feelings, allowing the dreamer to move on in life and to become consciously expressive in his current relationships. Whether he ever reconciles with his biological family or not can hardly be predicted, and is not necessary. What is crucial is how the dreamer relates in the present moment, and so the Dream Source uses the imagery from the past to evoke the dreamer to deep work in the present.

29

As a personal statement I can say there is no more moving work than going fully and emotionally into a dream's dynamics and evoking healing there. Through this and other work that evening, all of us men felt a wonderful energy and closeness as we expressed our masculine power within a context of relatedness. Basic, then, to all dreamwork is to bring resolution to the issues the dream presents, and it helps to do it within a supportive atmosphere.

SUMMARY

The world is in an outer and inner crisis today. The next great evolutionary step must involve the inner life in balance with the outer life by taking back projections and integrating them. Central to this shift will be the revival of dreamwork as a world cultural expression and healing. Dreams exist as an experience of potential and meaning from a source other than ego consciousness. We call this the Dream Source, the Self, the integrative centre within the psyches of all living people. The Dream Source speaks to us in the universal language of images, suggesting life principles to work with, showing us the nature of our projections, and revealing to us our inner patterns as well as the daily issues of our lives. Besides our problems, dreams also reveal new potentials for living meaningful lives by working with our dreams. Many people try to interpret their dreams instead of learning how to actualise them. Interpreting dreams keeps the ego in charge, whereas, what is needed is the conscious ego side of ourselves letting go to and actualising the deeper source within, the Self, the Dream Source. Dreams seem to present us most often with personality and life issues to resolve. In this sense the Dream Source wants healing. We participate in a healing process by doing dreamwork. This leads to resolution and personal change which allows us to live different and more healed lives in the present.

THINGS TO DO

Here we go again for some creative and committed responses. Please write to the following.

- What is your view of the world? Now what is your world view? What do you think is the basis of life? How do you see yourself as part of the next evolutionary step? Expand your view of things until you have a world view and can place your individual self in history.

- How committed are you to integrating your projections? What is your practice for integrating them?
- Describe in your own words what a dream is, and what dreamwork is.
- To see if you have the model down, or one of your own, describe how the dream originates and what place it has in our inner life. Do you remember the stages?
- Find a life principle in one of your dreams, or in a dream in this book. Is it in concept or imagery? How would you say it in your own words? What practice will you now do to live the principle in your everyday life? How is that for grounding?
- What is wrong and what is right about dream interpretation? What is dream interpretation versus dream actualisation?
- Take one of your recent dreams and actualise it in the outer life in some way. Write up your results in your dream journal. What? No dream journal yet? Or you are not using the one you have enough?
- To the extent you want to commit yourself and your time, list the issues raised in recent dreams. In fact, a basic task to do with every recorded dream is to write comments giving the issues raised by the dream. Now take one of your issues and work in a process which helps resolve that issue. You can simply write to the issue, or do any of the methods given in this book. Or go work with someone who can guide and support you in a process.

3 · THE DREAM EGO – THE YOU IN YOUR DREAM

True knowledge does not come through identifying with oneself but through becoming an object to oneself on a reality basis.

A man dreamed that a rattlesnake with bared fangs rose up in front of him a nose length away. He woke up and later in the dream group did a Guided Dream Re-entry with the experience in which he kept the image of the snake in his imagination and felt an incredible energy throughout his heart and body.

What is the thing of greatest value on earth that we can achieve? No, not any amount of money, not even a true love, whatever or whomever that turns out to be. Not even life itself. This is the paradox. *Life is for more than the living of life.* The one thing we can win if we work at it, this the Great Secret, is to become conscious by reflecting back upon ourselves in such a way we know a tremendous amount about us and about existence. Just as this is only a book until you work with its concepts and practises, so you are only a person until you work with You in such a way that you know yourself more than anyone else can know you. For this, the premier method for discovering one's ego, and therefore oneself, is Following the Dream Ego, a dreamwork method which can also be applied to how we go through other primary experiences in life. Many people feel they know themselves better than others know them, yet this is often defensive self-asserting. *True knowledge does not come through identifying with oneself but through becoming an object to oneself on a reality basis.*

What is the symbol most common to every dream? Many people answer all sorts of things, such as, water, the shadow, the child. Curiously, the uninitiated have little recognition it is themselves in the dream, the *dream ego*, the image of oneself, that is the most common symbol. Almost all dreamwork schools place little emphasis on the dream ego. It's as if the ego does not know ego exists. That's how identified we are with the outside world. We see everything as out there, little recognising the extent to which we are projected into our environment.

17. WE SYMBOLISE OUR WORLD TO USE IT AS A REFLECTION FOR OUR INNER SELVES.

What then is a symbol? It is an action or imagery which evokes and focuses energy from within a person. A symbol is a projection device. We can almost say everything out there we look at and engage in is symbolic, while at the same time being concrete. A *sign* is not a symbol but an image or action representing one central and direct meaning recognised by all. A traffic sign which says 'Stop' has the meaning, you are required by law to stop in your car before proceeding. That same traffic sign in a dream in your mother's bedroom will have many possible meanings to many people. Two sticks crossed hung on a wall are simply two sticks crossed to someone who is not a Christian. You think you know your love partner or your child. Yet do you know them as they are, or have you projected out on to them your inner parent or child, or other dynamics of the personality? Actions also have their symbolic functions. Love-making can be simple bodily release to some, while to others it represents love and unity.

As in life so in dreams. The psyche takes its symbol images from the exterior world. Love-making occurs in outer life and in dreams, symbolising a possibly unity experience yet also many things such as release, new birth, relationship, and even abuse. We work with dreams both *symbolically* and *literally*. We look at what the images and actions might symbolise by doing dream tasks with them. We also see what is literally there in the dream, its structures and issues.

In many dreamwork approaches people focus on other symbols in the dream besides the dream ego. They want to know what the elevator means, or the car crashing, or being overcome by a tidal wave. They ask, what is happening in your life that is like a tidal wave? and other questions like this. They leap off from the dream into the person's life. These approaches are not doing dreamwork, but interpreting dreams

33

by applying them to life and then trying to solve life's problems. No wonder the dream ego is neglected by almost everybody! So few know its role or importance in dreams and even in life.

18. THE KEY TO CONSCIOUS ENLIGHTENMENT IS THE DEVELOPMENT OF THE CREATIVE EGO.

It takes ego to find ego. The ego is the conscious side of the personality, the choice-making function, the consciousness which makes us aware and gives us a personal identity.

The Ego and its Dynamics

By looking at figure 4 we see the *ego* as one centre with its two opposite *direction arrows* representing *choice-making* and *consciousness*. Choice is choosing one direction and not another, a unique function of the ego. Consciousness is awareness plus appropriate action (it differs from simple awareness in that it is knowledge which causes action). The intellect is blended with feeling to cause choice and action. The ego is also seen as the centre of, and almost identical with, the conscious personality. We as conscious people make choices every day of our lives, and use *attitudes* as the context upon which to make those choices. Attitudes are usually unconscious contexts for choice. Closely allied with the ego is its *defence system*. It defends itself both against the world and against the unconscious. In order not to feel overwhelmed, that is, to lose its sense of personal identity, control, and choice-making power, the ego builds walls of attitudes and ways of behaving. This it will do and this it will not do. The defended personality tries to close itself to what feels threatening to it. These dynamics are repressed, creating the *shadow* which is hidden deep within the person and is unconscious. The shadow makes us do things we normally would not do, as in any compulsions we might have. To help the ego protect itself it also has besides the defence system its *persona*, the positive mask and behaviour the ego identifies with and shows to others to get along in the world.

Yet all the time impinging on the ego and its persona are strong forces in *relationship, the world,* and *spiritual destiny.* The ego would like to control these forces, but they are often at least as strong as it is. A better attitude of cooperation, and even yielding, is required, yet still keeping a sense of self and personal identity. Deep within the psyche resides the *Self Centre* and the various *archetypes.* These also have a profound influence on ego, so profound the ego can no longer stay in control. It needs to develop the *Ego – Self axis,* a committed relationship in which

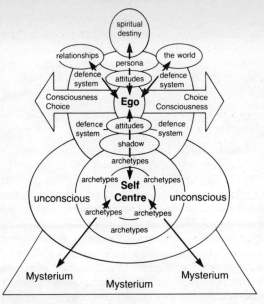

Figure 4 The ego and its dynamics showing its chief functions, points of identity, and its context to the rest of the psyche.

the Self balances the ego and the rest of the psyche, and the ego serves the Self through its choice-making and consciousness functions. And underneath and around it all is the *Mysterium*, that which is greater even than the unconscious or outer life, the unknown upon which the known rests, the transpersonal connection with the universe.

We practise humility by studying the ego in its proper relation to other dynamics which influence it. If we find our essential place and live it, then a deep fulfilment comes into our lives. All these dynamics are very much reflected in dreams, and one simple yet profound technique is to take the diagram and its dynamics and apply it directly to a dream by asking questions. Where is the Self Centre in my dream? and so on.

Following the Dream Ego

Perhaps the most original and outstanding method of the *Jungian-Senoi approach* to dreamwork is Following the Dream Ego, first devised in 1978. It is a conscious technique primarily of analysis, yet it lays the groundwork for the unconscious energy techniques of

Rewriting the Dream, Dream Re-entry, and Dialogueing with Dream Figures.

Following the Dream Ego is a dreamwork technique in which we look closely at what the image of ourselves in the dream is doing and not doing in interacting with the dream situation. First we describe the *actions*, then we infer the *attitudes* behind those actions which seem to govern them. We also look for *feeling reactions* on the part of the dream ego, either expressed or not expressed. In comparison with outer life we see what the appropriate feeling reaction might be and why the dream ego is or is not expressing this reaction. We also note the dynamics in other dream characters which could be, yet are not, expressed in the dream by the dream ego. We then go on to doing dreamwork, such as rewriting the dream with the dream ego this time asserting itself more and even taking on characteristics of other dream figures and seeing what happens. This work is then applied to outer life where the dreamer is encouraged to act more expressively or differently than usual, based on the dreamwork.

The advantage of following the dream ego in one's dreams is that seeing who one is and is not in the dream state helps one find one's fundamental identity. What an honest mirror we are to ourselves when we see how we are acting or not acting in our dreams!

19. THE MOST COMMON SYMBOL IN DREAMS IS THE DREAM EGO, THE IMAGE OF THE DREAMER.

The dream ego is usually the image of oneself in the dream. I say usually because sometimes in a dream we may experience the focus of our awareness and self-identity in someone else or even in some object.

Examples: A dreamer dreamed he was the knife and fork place setting at his parents' table. A woman dreamed she was a man. A dreamer dreamed he was quite a bit older than his present age. (One can also dream of oneself as being younger.)

20. THE DREAM EGO IS A POINT OF SELF-IDENTITY WITHIN THE DREAM.

Example: A young woman dreamed she was in a swivel chair high off the floor which felt precarious. Others in the room were questioning her. What are you doing there? How are you going to get down? Do you need help? She focuses and moves the chair in such a way she lowers it herself and reaches the floor. (Teaching dream in which the dream ego learns how to take care of itself rather than depend on others.)

Comment: In this dream the focus is on the dream ego as self-identity. Will the dreamer in the dream be effective by herself or need help? Does she know what she is doing there (indicating the need for self-awareness)? Will she take the necessary measures to come down to the floor and ground herself? In the end she meets the challenge and is successful, a good prediction as to how she will handle her life at this time.

In the following dream we see the dream ego, as an image of self-identity, going through an identity crisis – the possible loss of the known self in a process more powerful than the ego itself.

Example: A man jumps into the water. The first layer is clear and light blue. Then he starts sinking down into the other dark and denser layer. He lets himself go with it and does not wake himself up, knowing eventually he will sink so deeply he will be crushed into atoms.

Comment: On the surface this might seem like a dangerous dream portraying the fragmentation of the ego and the dreamer's inability to function in a sane and effective way. For some people disintegration imagery would indicate a need for caution, grounding, protection, and rigorous self-affirmation. In this case the dreamer accepted the dream as his ability to now go through a transformative process without due fear. Going below the surface into the depths of what would face him could well mean the disintegration of his known self-identity. In the dream state he was able to experience the process symbolically and understand its implications in terms of his individuation and transformation. He also enrolled in an ongoing dream group at this time.

Note in the dream he does not go through the disintegration, if that would occur. He is willing for it to happen as he reaches the depths, yet in terms of his inner life, who knows how the process will work? So building ego identity does not mean creating a rigid structure of images and attitudes to last for all time. *The ego in its pure form operates as the centre of awareness and choice-making.* In the growth process we work to give up rigid images of ourselves as well as rigid attitudes, values and beliefs. This gives us the flexibility to choose openly how to live life.

21. THE DREAM EGO OBSERVES OR ENGAGES IN ACTIVITY IN THE DREAM.

A fundamental distinction can be made as to whether you primarily *observe* the action in the dream, or *participate* in the action, or even *initiate* action, usually an advanced state in dreamwork. People who are primarily observers in their dreams include those who do not actively work with their dreams:

Example: A woman dreamed she was watching a gang of people attack her family and she did nothing. Dreamers who are just learning to write down their dreams will have mostly unresolved dreams in which they are watching the action. (Ego Issues dream pointing directly to dream ego behaviour.)

Observers also include those who are not actively engaged in a growth process. People who are minimally self-aware live life in largely routine and patterned ways. They seldom take an innovative or decisive role in major areas of their lives. They observe the action rather than place themselves at the centre of what is going on. How do you see yourself regarding this issue?

A fundamental life task

Analyse whether you are more on the side of observing life or directly participating in it. Find the areas in which you are thus one-sided and devise simple tasks to create new growth and balance.

Example: If you are primarily an observer give yourself the task of initiating something at least once a day, such as, for example, a conversation. By taking the initiative you will be making yourself a direct participant in your life. If however you are initiating and active all over the place, give yourself the task of waiting for things to happen while you simply observe what is going on. Will you be able to stand it? What anxieties or feelings are evoked? In terms of these two dynamics see how they come up in your dreams. Then do rewriting of certain dreams to create a balance between the two participating and observing functions.

22. A GOAL OF CREATIVE DREAMWORK IS TO DEVELOP IN THE DREAM STATE THE CAPACITY TO INTERACT FULLY WITH WHAT IS GOING ON.

Example: A woman dreamed her father was choking at the sink and she put her arms around his waist and pressed his diaphragm, expelling vomit, some of which got on to her. This saved him. She woke up excited by her action. She enacted this dream in the dream group to experience her feelings more directly and to change her behaviour. She also became more confronting and active with the men in her life.

The key formula for ego development

We start as observers of life, taking in what is going on. Then as we risk more we allow ourselves to become directly involved with the action. We participate. We act, and we react. Because we are involved in experiencing and not merely observing life we must react to things, making choices as we can, and coping as we go along. A further stage of development can then begin to manifest. We go from being reactive to becoming active. We anticipate. We initiate. We risk. We prepare. We intuit what will happen. We make choices which help situations change before they reach extreme states. *We have become active rather than reactive in life.*

In the above dream the woman is *reactive*, responding well to her father's crisis. Then in the dreamwork enactment she re-experiences being fully present. She is no longer the observer in life, as she has been in the past. She has come out of her shell. Yet dreamwork means becoming *active*, moving out of being *reactive*. Now for her life task she handles situations with men before they reach the extreme form symbolised in her 'father dream'. She is able to include more of life as she anticipates, risks, and enters into dealing with things creatively and with conscious choice. *The ego development formula is going from observer to reactor to actor in life.*

Excellent training methods for becoming active in dreams and life are Dream Re-entry, Rewriting the Dream, Following the Dream Ego, Dialogueing with Dream Figures, Dream Enactment, the Dream Task. We will be describing each of these techniques further, and they are all in Chapter 6 for quick reference. What is important here again is that we follow the dream itself. This dream has the dreamer quite active, motivated by an extreme event. Sometimes it takes extreme negative motivation. When a dreamer has this kind of dream we enact it if possible, so she gets it into her blood and bones. This gives her new ways of handling her life. Rewriting the Dream and Dream Re-entry would probably not have evoked as much energy as did the Dream Enactment. Dream Enactment was chosen because the dream itself was so full of energy and she liked strong feeling experiences, even though she was scared this first time to get that involved in one of her dreams. The goal is, *as in dreams, so in life. The more active we can be in life the better we create with its potential.*

39

23. TO MAKE SENSE OF ALMOST ANY DREAM, FOCUS ON WHAT THE DREAM EGO IS OR IS NOT DOING IN THE DREAM.

We do not need to know what a dream symbol means to experience it directly. We do not even need to focus on the dream symbols themselves to gain meaning from our dreams. Focus on what your dream ego is and is not doing in the dream for a rich experience in itself.

Example: It was winter in the dream and I was separated by an ice wall from where I was going. I tried to climb the wall and finally succeeded. (Teaching dream in which the dream ego is given a valid way to approach difficulties in life.)

Comment: We do not need to know what the ice wall symbolises or where the dreamer is going to realise a central aspect of this dream. The dreamer experiences herself overcoming a major obstacle regardless of what that obstacle is.

Common error: Typically dreamers like to know first what their symbols mean. They often fail to realise what they are doing in their dreams.

A creative action: The dreamer can use the above dream image for focus in dealing with difficult situations in her life. *The dream reveals the pattern and what to do about it. The waking ego carries out the creative action in outer life.* This is a fundamental formula for doing dreamwork. We again need to go over the nature of ego.

24. THE WAKING EGO IS THAT FUNCTION IN THE PERSONALITY WHICH MAKES CHOICES AND FOCUSES AWARENESS.

We analyse ego activity in the dream to see how the waking ego also functions or needs to function. The ego is not the full personality of an individual, although he or she may think so. Its job is to make choices and focus awareness without getting in the way of itself by trying endlessly to be in control of life.

Choice is directing energy in one direction and not another. Awareness is remembered feelings, images and concepts arranged with some sense of wholeness and pattern. *Attitudes are primarily unconscious contexts or statements about life* on the basis of which we make our choices.

Example: If I am often running from powerful forces in my dreams, then I probably have the attitude 'what I can't control is dangerous to me'. On the basis of this attitude I will choose to run from, or hide from, forces which I cannot control in the dream and in life. (Compensatory dream to the ego's waking attitude that either it needs to be in control or it is in control of its life.)

Fallacy: The assumption *what I cannot control will be harmful to me.* Realistically, only half the powerful forces in life will be dangerous and potentially destructive. Many powerful energies in life may benefit us if we let them.

Fallacy: That the best way to deal with life is to control it.

People try to control everything these days, their partners, their children, the government, the weather, even dreams. Many people do not like their dreams because they are hardly ever in control in them. Better to interact with and balance forces than try to overcome them or retreat from them.

As in dreams, so in life. The way we act in dreams may be a more accurate record of the way we act in life than our self-centred view of ourselves.

25. CHOICE IS DIRECTING ENERGY IN ONE DIRECTION AND NOT ANOTHER.

Many people tend to avoid choice-making by falling into routines. They eat the same foods, make love the same way night after night, and never make choices in their dreams. Note when you have a dream in which you are choosing for something important. A *choice point* is when you choose to go in one direction and not another. *When you begin having choice points in your dreams then you are developing your consciousness and choice-making.* Some dreams in which we may make a significant choice are likely to be compensatory to weak choice-making in outer life. The difference is Confirming dreams show you making the same choice in the dream after you have made it in outer life, thus affirming or enhancing, or even challenging, your new step. A Teaching dream may show you making a new choice as the next step. It usually comes after a series of Compensatory dreams in which you are challenged to new choice and action, yet do not come through.

Within the psyche, the inner workings of the personality, exists energy and the channels through which it moves. Most behaviour is instinctual, especially in other species besides man. This means the channels through which energy moves are so strong the organism must behave in a certain way.

Choice, however, is when we have the ability to direct energy in more than one channel. We can choose to eat or not eat a certain food, for instance. *If we can choose not to do something as well as to do it, then we have choice.*

Dreams are instinctual in the sense they show us the pattern of how a certain energy moves in us. Introducing choice into the dream state means the dreamer can in the dream choose to go one direction and not another, or carry out or not carry out some action.

Example: The dreamer is swimming in an ocean and starts to drown. She realises she is dreaming and can change the scene to get out of it. Instead, she remembers the author telling her to let go to the action in the dream. She chooses to let go to the waves and they carry her ashore. (Ego Issues and Teaching dream showing the ego choosing new behaviour in order to teach it to be less controlling in outer life.)

Comment: The dreamer has made a choice in the dream state and thus realises she can make choices. Yet she also realises she does not need to control the situation but can let go to it for healing. This is choice without control. We do not need to control things to choose what is best. *Always the first choice is to accept reality. The second choice is to interact with it.*

26. THE DREAM EGO MAY BEHAVE IN THE DREAM IN A SIMILAR OR A DIFFERENT WAY TO THE WAKING EGO IN OUTER LIFE

If your dream ego is acting in a similar way to the way you act in outer life then the dream may be confirming a pattern which you have. Also, this could show self-awareness on your part, as people who are not much aware will not recognise themselves in many of their dreams.

Example: The author, who had just written a book, was in his dream presenting himself and his approach to other professionals. (Confirming dream affirming what the dreamer was doing was fulfilling work.)

Comment: This was a Confirming dream which came after he did the work in outer reality, not before, in which case a dream would show potential and not actual, and be classified as a Prospective or Potentate dream. If your dream ego is acting differently from the way you see yourself normally acting in outer life, in a Compensatory dream, then the dream may be showing you behaviour or attitudes which you are not yet aware of because you are repressing them or have not made them conscious.

Example: In a series of dreams a young mother was yelling at and beating up her two small children. These dreams horrified her because in outer life she saw herself as very loving with her children. After dreamwork she realised she had been identified with being only a good mother and repressing her natural anger caused by taking care of small children. (Compensatory dream showing repressed feelings and issues not available to consciousness because the dreamer is identified with being the good mother.)

27. THE DREAM EGO MAY ACT DIFFERENTLY IN A DREAM FROM THE WAY IT ACTS IN WAKING LIFE SO AS TO EXPERIENCE NEW BEHAVIOUR FIRST IN THE DREAM STATE BEFORE TRYING IT OUT IN WAKING LIFE.

Example: A man in his thirties dreamed he had become a tiger who was threatening people. He came into a meeting of instructors and to protect himself he swatted each one down with his paw. He was surprised and upset at the power he showed, and upset as to why he had done what he had done in his dream. (Compensatory and Teaching dream showing a different attitude and persona from the waking one of the dreamer. Also the dream seems to be teaching him to use his power.)

Comment: This dreamer admitted in his outer life he was not at all assertive, ambitious, or outgoing. We used the method of contrasts in Objectifying dreams to get to what the dream's issues for him might be. As a tiger he was obviously powerful, assertive, and even dangerous. This contrasted with his outer image of himself as quiet and one who tends to go along with things. His outer life dream task was to imagine he was his dream tiger when going into situations challenging him to extend himself. This task excited him. We discover from this particular dreamwork a general principle: *We can express ourselves differently in life by embodying qualities we express in dreams.*

This is meaningful work, for obviously the Dream Source evaluates our behaviour and wants more from us than we presently express. By enacting dream energies we are serving the deeper Self and Dream Source. We are following an inner direction for our lives.

28. OUR DREAMS MAY SHOW BEHAVIOUR, ATTITUDES, OR POTENTIALS WHICH OUR INTEGRATIVE SELF WOULD LIKE TO SEE DEVELOPED FOR OUR WHOLENESS AND EFFECTIVENESS IN LIFE.

Example: A woman recently diagnosed as having breast cancer dreamed she saw a surgeon cut into her son's anus and it became too horrible to watch. She wanted to stop the surgeon yet felt helpless. (Teaching dream amplifying feelings and issues and what needs to be chosen.)

Comment: This dreamer was having a difficult time accepting the need for surgery and so the Dream Source put her in the situation which she most feared so she could experience fear and anger and work with it. Her decision to accept the knife came after struggling with the greater fear of losing her life. The Dream Source has her son being the recipient of the knife as if saying, you must treat your body as an object you love and do what is necessary to take care of it. Through her dream she was able to face her feelings about cancer and surgery, and then change her attitude and 'get on with it'. The result was successful surgery. With the loss of her breasts went the cancer. Her transformation from going through this experience using counselling and dreamwork led to seeing herself more spiritually and less physically, as in youth. She went on to a career of amazing creativity and still had intimate relationships!

29. DREAM EGO ACTIVITY IN THE DREAM REFLECTS UNDERLYING ATTITUDES TOWARDS LIFE.

Attitudes are the unconscious contexts out of which we make our choices.

How to transform attitudes

Working consciously, we *discover* our unconscious attitudes, and how they affect our behaviour, *test* them as to how realistic or meaningful they are, and then *choose* whether to keep them as conscious principles for living life, ot to *substitute* new principles for old attitudes.

Example: In her dream a mother was trying to get her thirteen-year-old son to put on his trousers. His genitals were showing yet he didn't see the point of covering himself. His attitude was it didn't matter what others thought. Then he was told an older boy he admired had come to visit him. He ran to his room and put on his jeans. (Ego Issues dream highlighting a major attitude for the dreamer to deal with in herself and possibly in her son.)

Comment: We begin to wonder whose dream this is. For in it we have the boy himself going through an attitude change from 'I don't give a damn about what others think' to 'I care how I look and what certain people think of me'. The mother was more focused on her son than on herself. Her attitude towards her son was to see him as a problem (negative motivation). We helped her connect to her basic attitude about herself as seeing herself always as a problem. The attitude is, *the way to live life is to fix its problems.* Gradually in dream group she was able to focus on positive motivations and attitudes regarding herself, her son, and life.

There are two great motivations in life: positive and negative. You can either see each situation as a possibility for disaster or as a potential for new life.

30. FEELINGS IN DREAMS ARE OFTEN CREATED BY ATTITUDES, NOT ATTITUDES BY FEELINGS.

The fundamental issue is, on what basis do we make our choices? Some choose rationally, following certain attitudes or ethics which are part of an identity they have adopted. Others do not know what they follow, being mainly reactive rather than active in life. Still others follow their feelings. They see themselves as having gut reactions. They either feel to do something or not to do it. They either like something or dislike it. Those who choose feeling may think they have based their actions on who they are, yet this can be questioned.

When we look closely at the dream ego we can see that, more often than not, attitude produces feeling, and not the other way round. *If we change our attitudes we will change our feeling reactions to things.* The origin of an attitude often lies in an emotional experience like a trauma or a great pleasure. We cannot simply change an attitude through will power. We will have to go through the emotions related to the original trauma (the carthartic method) to change our pattern and our attitude.

Example: An attractive twenty-eight-year-old woman dreamed that two older brothers were calling her a slut and other names. This brought tears to her eyes in telling the dream. In the dream itself she had fought with her brothers, trying to define for herself her sexuality and what was right for her. The dream scene reminded her of what her older brothers had done to her as she was entering puberty. (Ego Issues Dream highlighting attitudes to be dealt with.)

Comment: This dream episode obviously produces strong feeling. What is the attitude represented by the brothers' remarks? That being sexually expressive as a woman is a bad thing? Thus the attitude itself made her feel badly and produced the tears. We also see the dreamer trying to oppose the attitude represented by the brothers' behaviour with an opposite attitude and behaviour. In the dream she defends herself, and behind the action is the attitude *she has the right to express her sexuality in a healthy manner.* However, another question lurks in the dream. Is she expressing her sexuality in ways which create fulfilling relationships? Do the brothers represent a negating side of herself or a moral evaluation of herself, perhaps in distorted form? She also told us in childhood her brothers had been companions until she started puberty, and then they teased her and rejected her.

The dreamwork: We did not take sides yet helped the dreamer become aware of the various issues raised by her dream, including crying and anger as she told us about her childhood. This was her catharsis, the releasing of pent-up feelings from the past. Some positive attitudes to come out of this work were:

- I am the only one who can define and evaluate my own sexuality.

- I do not need to defend myself when someone else criticises me.

- What other people say about me may have little to do with me and much to do with them.

- I can learn to separate myself out from men's projections onto me.

- I have a right to feel my sexual feelings while making love rather than be focusing so much on the man, making him feel good.

Each of these attitudes will be likely to produce positive feelings instead of negative ones. Some of the attitudes behind the negative feelings produced by the dream are:

- I am a bad person because I am sexual.

- When someone criticises me or is terrible to me, they must be right.

- Men should not hurt women.

- I cannot handle men who try to hurt me.

- Women should please men or they will be hurt or left.

We can see how each of these attitudes would stimulate tears and anger. *Change your attitude and you change your emotional reaction to an event*. The Dream Source presents the issue, not the solution in this case. Dreamwork amplifies the issue, getting to her repressed feelings. Then we do Following the Dream Ego to get to the old unconscious attitudes and to the new attitudes which will help create fulfilment.

It can be dangerous to follow your feelings in making a choice when you do not know what attitudes are producing those feelings.

Attitudes are rules produced by our unconscious reactive patterns to previous life events. We are hurt and produce an attitude justifying closing off to life as it is. Why function in the present on the basis of how you functioned in the past? Get to your feelings in making choices. Then go one step further to the attitude behind the feeling. *True freedom is knowing what unconscious attitudes are determining your reactions in a given situation.* If you know your attitudes you have conscious choice whether to fulfil them or not.

Summary

In Following the Dream Ego we may first look and see what attitudes are embedded in the dream, or we may get to the feelings involved and then to the attitudes behind the feelings. We may use earlier experiences when we felt the same way to help show us how it all started and what attitudes were created back then which are still unconsciously governing us today. Then we create new attitudes which motivate us to cope with the dream situation more positively. We ask, how could you have handled this differently? What attitude about yourself would you need to deal with these adversarial brothers of yours? Then we might do Rewriting the Dream or Dream Re-entry, yet this time having the dream ego operate from an affirming set of attitudes. The end result would be a healing experience rather than a negating one. We next ask for a commitment from the dreamworker to live similar outer situations with the new set of attitudes. Even though people may act in the outer as they do in the dream, the dreamer can change her approach and achieve fulfilling results with new and more positive feelings.

31. FEELINGS IN DREAMS CAN ALSO BE INHERENT AND NOT ATTITUDE BASED

Example: The author dreamed he was taking care of a two-year-old boy. At one point they had separated and came running together, both feeling an open-armed joy at finding each other. (Expressive dream in which the action expresses natural feeling and action for the sake of the experience itself.)

Comment: Feeling is energic reaction, positive or negative. Energy goes towards or away from an object. We either like or dislike something. All feelings seem to be variations on this dynamic, and so we have what Jung has called the *Feeling Function* inside us. The feeling in the above dream seems to be based on a natural bonding reaction rather than on some hidden attitude. Yet then again, the feeling of relief might have arisen out of the release of fear produced by an attitude *being alone in life leaves one more unprotected than if one were with someone*. Quite possibly feelings and attitudes always go together. One is energic, one conceptual, as two sides of the same dynamic.

32. FALLING ASLEEP IS THE WAKING EGO LETTING GO OF ITS AWARENESS AND CHOICE-MAKING POWERS.

Falling asleep means letting go of ego consciousness and control. Many people experience *hypnogogic* images (image flashes) at this time, indicating that the images of the inner life rather than those of the outer life are coming to the fore. *Sleep* is a letting go of ego fixation on the outer which allows the inner life to come into awareness through dreaming. We need to sleep and dream to process what is happening to us in ourselves and in life. In the three to five dreams we have each night, whether we remember them or not, our Dream Source is processing our life with us, for us. Consciousness means making this unconscious process conscious through dreamwork so we may bring choice and creativity to the process. This changes the automatic, somewhat integrative process from *reactive* to *interactive* with startling and vitalising results.

33. DREAMWORK PRESENTS THE OUTER WORLD AS A SYMBOLIC ARENA WITHIN

Most people's egos identify with outer life. They see their experience as 'out there'. When they are having a relationship problem they may see the problem as the other person rather than something from inside themselves they are projecting onto the person. People identify themselves as Americans, Catholics, Blacks, and so on, yet what does this mean? How we feel and think as persons is determined primarily on our inner experiences and not on where we live, what church we worship in, or the colour of our skin. People have identity problems because they try to identify with outer things which do not satisfy the longing to find oneself as a person with individuality and inner experience.

What this means is that dreamwork can help you develop the *inner life*, the felt world of dynamic experience. A major aspect of the dreamwork process is disidentification from the outer world so we may relate to it creatively without being driven by our identifications.

Why else does the Dream Source take as its universal language of imagery the images and actions occurring in the outer? Have you ever dreamed of anything which did not exist in any way in the outer? Of course not. No one dreamed of an automobile before they appeared on the roads. In the same way we cannot dream of the future. We can image composites of the way things will look based on present realities. Yet to see something totally new in a dream? Is that possible?

34. THE DREAM SOURCE DOES NOT WANT THE DREAMER OR THE DREAM EGO TO CONTROL THE DREAM.

The issue of who controls what in life or in dreams is a major one. Out there in the dreamwork movement and in the spiritual movement are people attempting to control their dreams by changing them once they become 'conscious' in the dream state. This focus is in contrast to the fact that most people's dreams seem unresolved, showing the dream ego unable to control what is happening. *Most dreams can be seen as challenges by the Dream Source to give up attempting to control, and instead serve the Self, the centre within.* This statement contrasts with the view that dreams are unresolved because the dreamer is not skilled in controlling dreams or life.

Fundamental to personal growth and spiritual practice is to give up control in order to serve the sources of life in a process of actualisation. If you want to separate out the creative from the destructive, the good from the bad, in religious, psychological, and spiritual groups, look to who is trying to control things. Is the Zen master making his students meditate a certain way, or tripping them up at every juncture in which they think they have found the right path? Is the minister or priest serving the people and God, or is he teaching dogma and orthodox practice? Is the psychologist or educator dominating the client or supporting the client in his or her process?

Our demons symbolise all those forces which we cannot control.

At various times in our lives we may be afraid of life and of even falling asleep at night. Fear of falling, beyond what is natural, may be based on repressed feelings. As egos we seek to control life rather than relate to it. This leads to repression of things which are outside our control. Then at night in letting go into sleep the demon repressions come out to haunt us in our dreams and anxiety symptoms, such as teeth grinding and bad breath.

49

*Example:*A man dreamed he descended into the basement of a house and there encountered a witch who went after him when he tried to leave. Finally he turned and faced the witch with his determination to fight. He made angry sounds back at her, and then woke up. (Teaching dream in which the ego is being shown the basic dreamwork principle, to relate to your adversary's energy, take it on, and express it yourself.)

*Comment:*Yes, the demon came up when the dreamer let go of control. The normal unconscious pattern for many people is to repress certain things which become personified in dreams as witches, demons, and the like. In the above dream the man, who was also a lawyer, had let go of control in falling asleep and then experienced the witch energy which he proceeded to flee from. Then he made a choice, turned, and himself embodied the energy he was originally afraid of. This is advanced dreaming which usually only a skilled person already consciously working on him or herself could come up with. Many untrained people will not only repress certain adversarial dynamics of life in an attempt to control them, but will go on to flee from those dynamics they cannot control. *A conscious commitment to wholeness means facing all aspects of one's psyche and of life.*

For contrast we have this dream example from a contemporary writer on lucid dreaming, Stephen LaBerge, as reported in his book on the subject. *Lucid dreaming* is a sleep state in which the dreamer wakes him or herself in the dream by realising a dream is being experienced and not an outer life situation. Practitioners of lucid dreaming develop the 'skill' of being aware they are dreaming. Once lucid they often go on to change the dream's imagery.

Example: In a dream Stephen LaBerge encountered some enemies, and would have fled from them, yet he recognised he was awake in his dream. He then approached the threatening figures to see what would happen, aware he did not have to feel fear since it was only a dream. (Ego Issues dream pointing to the lack of courage, commitment to remaining present no matter what, on the part of the dreamer in letting go of control.)

Which dream ego behaviour from the last two examples do you prefer? Which is the more healthy, the more enabling in dealing with life?

Again, we have the issue of control. In the first of our two examples the dreamer did not feel in control and tried to escape. Then he was contained and had to face the witch and deal with it, using some of its energy, and symbolising the repressed energy in the dreamer. We know this because of anger work done with the dreamer in his dreamwork. He cannot control the dream yet he can actively participate in it. He does not get rid of feelings natural to an adversarial situation as a way of dealing with it.

By contrast, the lucid dreamer cuts himself off from natural feeling by training himself to see dreams as imaginary and different from outer life and therefore nothing to be frightened of. The Self and Dream Source then loses the ability to present adversarial situations to the dreamer, and thus to the waking ego, so the dreamer can deal with fear and take on adversarial figures and situations without trying to control them. The lucid dreamer changes the adversarial situation by exerting control over the dream. This way of doing things has a direct bearing on living outer life as well.

The degree of congruence between inner and outer life indicates health or split personality dynamics.

This is of course an assertion and not a rigorously proven fact. Yet my own and others' clinical observations lead us to feel *health* is congruence and *illness* is opposition and disintegration in the relationship between parts.

The dream control person attempts to change difficult dream situations into pleasant ones. If this method were used in outer life, say in an argument, it would lead to the person saying to himself, and maybe others, this conflict is not real so I do not have to feel bad about it, and I can do whatever I want with it. A real conflict is real, is dangerous, can evoke legitimate fear, make the person face the issues as they are and deal with them, not by closing one's eyes but by opening them wider. Lucid dreaming seems still one more attempt to make things seem positive which are not positive in life. Training yourself to control your dreams, if it ever actually works, endangers you by making it harder for you to deal with reality as it is, not as you would like it to be.

A better way

Do not practise dream control but dream activity. Consider the dream and its situations as being just as real as outer situations. This is the normal state for dreaming. *Emotionally, dream situations are just as real as outer situations.*

Dreams can evoke issues and strong feelings. Our goal is not to lessen those feelings but to enhance them and to cope creatively with

51

them. The Dream Self presents scary situations so the dream ego can learn to deal with them directly, and thus also strengthen the waking ego in its encounter with life. Disengagement from life by cutting off your feelings is not the way to deal with things. Lucid dreaming, a phenomenon in itself, has little place in conscious dreamwork. Do not attempt to change your dreams. Actualise them!

Religions and adversity

Those religions which have adversarial figures such as Satan in Christianity or demons in Tibetan Buddhism may be repressive religions rather than integrative. This is highlighted when looking at the dreams of the religious which have their full share of adversarial dream symbols. Yet then again, everyone has dream adversaries. No religion seems able to include and integrate on an equal footing the adversarial aspects of life and personality. They always have a hierarchy of the good and the bad. *Dreams know no hierarchy.* We dream on forever the major dynamics of life and how we are or are not dealing with them. *A religion is a collective dream which needs waking from.* Tibetan religion goes so far as to state an advanced adept would no longer have dreams or dream images because they are awake when they are asleep. Their daytime consciousness goes right through the night. I doubt if this is so, yet if it is, what a price to pay in lost dreams for the light of a rarefied consciousness! More likely is that the dream-making source has been consciously destroyed through meditative practices so the 'masters' do not have to face and integrate the dark side. This is something we all have a tendency to do, especially if we are biased towards the positive.

The ego, in attempting to control life, exerts power to produce pleasant and positive experiences and to repress or avoid negative and suffering experiences. *Often what we call suffering is the ego feeling forced by adversarial forces to let go of controlling life.* Better to choose to let go of control rather than be forced to it. The fallacy is in affirming one side of life, the ego's, while denying the other side of life. *Dreams are more whole than we are as waking beings.* A series of dreams will include both the dark and the light. Why not do likewise?

Example: A woman dreamed she was sitting in the woods with her husband when a snake came towards them. Her husband moved out of the way yet she stayed quietly there to encounter the snake. It crawled up her and she got the feeling it wanted her to open her mouth. When she did the snake crawled in and coiled itself there with its head jutting out. She was very still. Then the snake crawled back down and went away. She realised she had been initiated and could talk with birds and little animals. (Great dream with major imagery and dream ego participation like going through an ancient rite.)

Comment: Many of us have dreams in which snakes or other animals come and want to bite us, especially when we are afraid of them. Here the dreamer deals with a potentially dangerous situation, the dark side, and a healing occurs. She can face the Power alone, do what it wants, and survive. She does more than survive. She yields control, yet not presence, and is initiated. She can communicate with birds and animals. She is in tune with nature by yielding consciously to the natural forces of life. What a beautiful dream of wholeness, of encompassing the light and the dark! She made several choices in the dream. She as dream ego was tested and passed the test, the initiation. She received the gift of tongues, the ability to communicate with fundamental life forces. She gave up control for relation to the energy. A year later her marriage broke up and then she had to go through a complete letting go process. Events happened which were severely outside her control. She went through this experience with tremendous suffering and spiritual growth. The dream snake often seems to signal destiny or 'the intervention of the other'. As in the Garden of Eden myth, the snake intervenes to catalyse a fundamental change in the status quo.

Consciousness is the paradoxical integration of the observing and the participating functions.

Example: In a famous Great dream the Swiss psychologist, C. G. Jung, dreamed he had come to a chapel high on a mountain. Inside in front of the flowers on the altar there sat in lotus position a yogi meditating with his eyes closed. Jung in the dream recognised the yogi was dreaming Jung and when he awoke Jung would be no more. (Great dream showing a spiritual reality, or leap in consciousness on the part of the dreamer.)

Comment: Jung is participating in life while another part of him, the central Self, is giving him the potentials to be realised. Jung observes this and recognises when he is perceived consciously by the dream Self, he will have lived his life and be no more in death. Quite a precarious position for any of us to be in! We think we are in control yet perhaps something somewhere knows us a lot better than we know ourselves, directs our activities, and has our fate in its hands? This is the Self, the source of dreams.

35. OUR ONE GOAL IN TRANSFORMING LIFE INTO MEANING IS TO DEVELOP A CONGRUENT AND VITALISING RELATION TO LIFE CENTRES WITHIN AND WITHOUT.

The two greatest causes of illness may be *one-sidedness* and *ego inflation*. *Health* is when the body and the mind are in balance. At some point the ego can make a fundamental choice to choose wholeness rather than ego-control and personality one-sidedness.

In terms of dreams, many dreams put the dream ego under a challenge of some sort. In dreams the dream ego is rarely in control. These dream tests result in typical reactions on the part of the dream ego:

- The dream ego remains the passive observer.
- The dream ego attempts to run from or hide from adversarial forces.
- The observing ego wakes the dreamer up to get the dream ego out of a scary situation.
- The lucid dream ego attempts to control the dream through lessening its emotional impact by calling it only a dream and therefore not real.

To take creative action the dream ego can:

- Keep itself in the dream as long as possible and see what happens.
- Change its point of view in the dream and accept the situation and then deal with it.
- Face adversarial forces and interact with rather than run from them.
- Express feeling reactions in the dream to what is happening.

The dream actualisation approach

By regularly doing dreamwork with your dreams and living aspects of them in daily life you will be an active and value-seeking dreamer. Your activity in the dream itself will increase. You will be interacting with dream characters and situations more fully and in harmonising ways. More of your dreams will reach resolution while in the dream state. You will occasionally experience *Great Dreams*, dreams of intense feeling and emotion with important resolutions in them and much insight as to their application to life. You will become one who is waking up to life.

Example: A woman dreamed she is running up hill from a dangerous figure who is about to get her. She knows if she reaches a house at the top of the hill with people there she has a chance to escape. She keeps going and the people at the top tell her to go into the house and out the back way and then she will be safe. On the first floor she encounters two doors, one of them numbered. She goes through the numbered door and climbs stairs to the second floor. Again she chooses to go through the numbered door and must climb another flight of stairs. On the third floor she asks the people about the two doors. They tell her she has been choosing the known because she is afraid of the unknown. She decides to open the unknown door, knowing she can leave the house through either door. (Teaching Dream giving major life wisdom.)

Comment: This dream came to someone who was beginning the dreamwork process. We see the dream ego is first motivated by negative motivation, the flight from that which might destroy it. Negative motivation is what pushes us to new behaviour in life. We are afraid of worse things happening to us and so we move and change. Then in this house of transition the dream ego confronts its normal pattern of making life choices. It chooses the known way as the safer way, implying the attitude *staying with the known is better than opening up to the unknown*. Yet is it? Perhaps this attitude is hardly realistic or one which leads to a full and dynamic life? She finally on the third try chooses to go through the unmarked door to the unknown. This is the choice, to choose mystery rather than certainty. To go where one has never been to find new life. Now her attitude can change to: *it is better to seek new life by breaking out of old patterns*.

SUMMARY

The symbol most common to our dreams is the dream ego, the image of ourselves in the dream. Through the dream ego we can see what kind of identity we have, how we operate in dreams and in life, and how to discover our unconscious attitudes, or laws which govern our behaviour. We note that sometimes the dream ego's behaviour is similar to the person's waking behaviour and sometimes different. We can understand from dream ego work how we choose and act, and we can also see how to change and improve ourselves and our actions. The Dream Source itself seems to portray the dreamer behaving in new and creative ways in a dream to get us to consider enacting that behaviour also in our waking lives. Thus by following how our dream ego is and is not behaving in our dreams we can learn about ourselves and how to improve our lives. Through dream ego work we learn about our self-identity, our attitudes, our feelings, and how we do or do not make choices. We also see how we relate or do not relate to other beings, inner and outer. In addition, because we ourselves are in our dreams we can experience a wide range of human emotions and situations. It is as if the dream itself becomes a symbolic arena for re-enacting and pre-enacting life. The dream is a great rehearsal place for dealing with the many aspects and issues of our existence. We get to deal specifically with fear, with choice-making, with violence and anger, with sexual energy, with sickness and health, with humour and joy. Yet one of the difficulties of becoming aware of oneself in the dream is that we may try to control our dreams and manipulate them, the so-called lucid dreaming experience. To become 'awake' in our dreams and to consciously control the imagery may give one a sense of being greater than other things in dreams or in life. This causes a lack of congruency between waking and dream life, possibly damaging the psyche. It may also bias or contaminate the image-making function used by the integrative centre in the psyche, which is attempting through dreams to convey messages and meaning to ego-consciousness without contamination by ego control. Ultimately health and wholeness seems to reside with those who do not seek to control their dreams yet to work actively with them, both in the dream state and by applying dream wisdom and energy to life, thus creating congruency between inner and outer life.

THINGS TO DO

- What do you know about yourself in terms of the world? What specifically are, or have been, your projections on to people and situations out there? What then is projection, and how are you currently integrating projections?

- Describe your creative ego and your self-centred ego. Make a list of characteristics about each. Why do we need creative ego?

- Describe your dream ego, at least in one dream. What is it doing and not doing? What are its attitudes? How is your dream ego different from your waking ego, or similar to it?

- How are you an observer in life and in dreams?

- How are you a participator in life and in dreams?

- How are you active rather than reactive in life and in dreams?

- Note which characteristics your dream ego has in a dream or two. Then see what dynamics are embodied in other dream characters.

Now take one positive and one negative dynamic of theirs and have the dream ego embody it doing Rewriting the Dream or even Dream Re-entry. What results? See how in your outer life you as waking ego can express a characteristic from a dream character not now being expressed in your life.

- What are the feelings being expressed or not expressed in your dream or series of dreams? What attitudes may be behind these feelings? What attitudes need changing, and to what? If you are not having feelings, what are you doing to relate to things and people?

- What is your pattern and how does it bring up the issue of control and letting go for you?

- Describe your control issues in life and in dreams. What happens when you let go of control and interact, if you have ever done this? What are your fears around control? What is the reality?

- If you choose to give up trying to control life and dreams, what can you substitute for it? Describe a commitment you will make to following the Dream Source rather than simply reacting to it or trying to control it. What does this mean you will try and do in every dream?

4 · Dreams and Relationship

We are in relationship with another to be able to find ourselves better.

A young woman dreamed she and her boyfriend started making love in a room where others could see what they were doing.

Relationship is both a vale of tears and a wild bed of wonderful feelings, the hidden voice of the lost child and the dancing joy of the wondrous child, the caring and responsible adult and the adult lost and adrift in a hard and difficult life.

Most of us live within the circle of relationship yet feel somewhat lost in it. After the experience, what have you? Where is the meaning, the routine is certainly there? And those who hook up together give wonder to their friends with the degree of incongruity exposed. We become both the crying parent and the responsible child. We marry our parents because we never graduated from childhood. We seek in adult life that which we never had as a kid. And in the long haul we project our longing on each potential partner, make connections and lose many more, and ask finally, what is it all for? We cannot have a completely fulfilling relationship and we cannot stand not to have it either. We exist in paradox, and have nowhere to turn but our dreams. The real dreams do not exist in fantasy but come to us each night of our lives with even more certainty than a lover might come to our beds.

Greater than relationship then, and Ah! the good, the sweetness, that happens there, is the quest for fulfilment. If relationship is not

58

the ultimate all the popular songs make it out to be, then where do we find the deep consummation which gives food to the soul?

Again, we look to our dreams. Whatever is inner is also outer, and whatever is outer is also inner. The conscious journeyer learns to nurture an inner relationship to him or herself at the same time he or she is creating anew the outer relationship. By working with our dreams around relationship issues we will be learning about ourselves and life. We are in relationship to companion another and to integrate within ourselves whatever teachings the relationship evokes. Just as dreams teach us the deepening process of life, so will relationships teach us if we do not close off to them. For both arenas we have the knowledge and techniques for doing the work. Here we shall focus on using dreamwork to integrate what is evoked in relating to another human being. By doing the work we shall learn more about ourselves and become more effective and understanding relators.

36. OUTER AND INNER RELATIONSHIPS ARE A MAJOR ARENA FOR DREAMWORK ACTIVITY.

As we have already observed, those who are starting to record their dreams do not interact in many of their dreams. Their dream egos are observers to what is going on in dream time. Through dreamwork we develop the ability to fully interact with whatever is happening in the dream. This change in inner life behaviour will be reflected in outer life behaviour. They will react to situations, yet how often will they consciously act by taking the initiative in establishing or changing a relationship?

Example: A man watched in his dream as another man came to the door and took his wife out for a date. He woke wondering if he was angry. (Ego Issues dream questioning the dreamer's ability to express feeling in himself or in relationship because his approach to life seems to be mainly as an observer.)

Comment: True feeling leads to action. If you feel something intensely, energy is flowing through you and you must act. Here in this dream the dreamer would have to leave his non-relational observer role and risk getting involved with his wife and whomever else wanted to relate to her. Very interesting! The Dream Source presents another figure and not the dream ego who wants the relationship. Need we say more, gentlemen!

37. DREAMS WILL SOMETIMES SHOW OUR NEEDS AND DIFFICULTIES IN RELATING.

Example: A man dreamed at first he was the executioner, the one who pulls the lever releasing the poisonous gas pill. He did this and a mist formed. Then the man he executed was no longer there, and the dreamer realised he himself had been executed. He cried out for help, by writhing on the ground. No one seemed concerned. He told them to get doctors and finally two came who tried to inject him with the antidote to the poison. They seemed incompetent and could not get the needle into his arm. He told them to let his wife do it. She was a nurse and could do it right. She injected him with the antidote and he was healed. (Ego Issues Dream reflecting certain attitudes needing to be made conscious.)

Comment: The dreamer said this dream reflected his being a loner before he married his present wife. Marrying her had saved his life and given him purpose. In working with him the author pointed to how the dreamer had moved into the role in the dream of being the wounded one needing help, and did he have an attitude that he had to do everything himself because others would goof it up? This rang true. He recognised that in his present relationship he could be vulnerable and trust that someone would be there for him when he needed her the most. The new growth for him was in letting go of his competent, controlling side to be interdependent with others. Both he and his wife were in dreamwork training together and sometimes the action got hot and heavy, as well as leading to new intimacy, anger, and caring.

38. DEFENSIVE DREAM RELATIONSHIPS CAUSE CONFLICTS.

Needing to defend oneself in a dream places one in conflict with adversaries. This seems obvious, and it is, yet what it suggests is that conflicting relationships also need resolving. This can come about if defensiveness is transformed. In this next example the dream ego is under attack and almost becomes a victim. She fights back, even though to wound or kill someone, even in a dream, is horrible to her. Fighting back increases the intensity of the relationship. The victim refuses to be victimised. She feels power in asserting herself, and then through Dream Re-entry she becomes reconciled with the adversary, taking on the power for creative use. Negative power changes to positive power.

Example: A woman dreamed a handsome young man was being

attacked by a wild woman who was trying to kill him. They struggled over possession of the knife. He was wounded yet got the knife away, becoming the image of the dreamer in the process. Now the dreamer had to keep the woman off. She realised with horror she would have to use the knife on her attacker because the attacker would not stop. The dreamer stabbed the adversary in the shoulder, and that ended the dream action. (Ego Issues dream highlighting the dreamer's need for a stronger masculine to protect herself.)

Comment: The woman did a Guided Dream Re-entry with this dream. Her adversary turned into her mother and she realised a childhood pattern was being evoked. She needed her strong inner masculine to prevent this adversary from taking over the way her mother did in her childhood. The end result of the Dream Re-entry was that they were reconciled. This meant to the dreamer she could move ahead and realise some of her goals without first getting criticised or adversarial. A second principle also emerges from this dreamwork.

Contemporary difficulties in relating are often based on relational patterns set up in childhood or early adult years.

The present relationship evokes a previous one. The healing comes from working on the previous relationship as an inner experience. This is usually done through dreamwork. Outer reconciling work can sometimes be accomplished with parents and former partners yet this is not necessary to heal inner splits and traumas. Another key principle central to dreamwork is: *You cannot heal yourself through outer work alone. You must heal the inner to change the outer. Inner healing changes you within so you can act differently out there.*

39. DREAM RELATING MAY SET THE STAGE FOR LIFE TRANSITIONS IN RELATIONSHIPS.

In the following example the dreamwork led this attractive thirty-one-year-old woman to consider marriage to her current man-friend. The Dream Source seems to have a level of attunement with major transitions in our lives, suggesting there is a destiny dynamic which asserts itself from the central archetype of the Self.

Example: The dreamer dreamed her ex-husband wanted her to go up in a helicopter with him. She was hesitant, yet when he put his arms around her she went. Her husband wanted to show her how much fun it was. The pilot raised the helicopter off the ground and the husband held the dream ego hanging outside the door. Once up she enjoyed the thrill of the ride. (Ego Issues dream helping the dreamer face her issues around a present relationship.)

Comment: In discussing her dream the young woman was asked to describe how she saw the relationship in the dream, especially her part in it. She recognised she was giving up control in letting herself be dangled out of the helicopter door. She had to trust both her ex-husband and the pilot. She realised the pilot was the one she trusted and so it was all right to be held by her ex-husband. In outer life it had been an early marriage which lasted three years. She had become stronger since then and able to take care of herself as an adult. Her present relationship of two years was a balanced and loving one, she felt. When it was suggested her dream might also be bringing up the issue of marriage she sucked in her breath and said that was a scary issue for her yet one she had already been thinking about. Sucking in her breath was like rising up in a helicopter, as is trusting a relationship enough to let go of needing to control it. The dreamer felt this was an important issue to have been raised by her dream. The work suggests the following relationship principle as it applies to life.

A full commitment to a relationship can only be based on a realistic assessment that you can trust yourself and the other person enough to let go of needing to control the relationship and the other person in it.

40. INNER DREAM RELATIONSHIPS ARE VALUABLE IN THEMSELVES.

Example: A woman dreamed she was making love with a sensitive male figure who knew exactly what to do to please her. He was in tune with her feelings and she felt the full experience of his presence with her, even after she was awake. (Expression dream for experiencing feelings not realistically possible in a present relationship. Not a Compensatory dream since the dreamer is conscious of what she does not have in her marriage and does not expect otherwise in the outer.)

Comment: The dreamer did not have a lover who was sensitive to her needs and so felt the happiness which came with her dream relationship. It could be said she was engaging in *wish fulfilment*, the wanting something you do not have. However, she was having an emotionally healthy experience full of love and warmth without needing to have an actual sensitive lover loving her. This may seem unreal, yet only to people identified with outer things. She had a full feeling experience, and that is what counts. The author has had many love experiences in the dream state, especially when no one was available for such a sharing in the outer.

41. RELATING TO STRANGERS IN DREAMS INVOLVES CONTACTING UNKNOWN ENERGIES WITHIN OURSELVES.

Some dream theorists would say *all parts of a dream are aspects of oneself*. With any dreamwork statement it is best to take an open stance. At one level everything in a dream may be reflecting ourselves. Yet at other levels any aspect of a dream can refer to an aspect of *outer life*, or to some *psychic attunement* with another person. We always look at every dream as possibly representing inner dynamics and outer dynamics.

Common fallacy: Many people new to dreamwork automatically think of a dream figure or situation as representing an outer figure or situation. This is the *fallacy of externalising one's unconscious*. To understand ourselves we must see things as almost always originating within.

Example: A dreamer dreamed the author was in her dream and she took the opportunity to ask him a question. His answer was she should get involved in the process of life and give up questioning it. This is what she thought the author in waking life would say also. (Teaching dream in which the dreamer receives wisdom from an inner part of herself.)

Comment: In the dream group I will often not directly answer people's questions, such as what does this symbol mean? This pushes the students back on themselves to look within and find their own responses to their issues. In the above dream example the dreamer is consulting her inner dream group leader. The answer she desires comes from her own source rather than an external source. Thus she is able to contact inner wisdom represented by the dream group leader.

One of the goals of dreamwork is to help people become proficient in contacting inner resources instead of seeking perspective from external people and philosophies. A major transition in the life journey is when a person can go from relying on external authorities and teachings to living from internal wisdom sources.

Major fallacy: That one can live a fulfilling life by putting one's faith in external teachings, doctrines, or wisdom figures and teachers. These 'crutches' are only good for the beginning stages. At least by midlife, journey people will be developing practices which enhance and make known internal source energies for dealing meaningfully with life.

42. RELATING TO A STRANGER IN A DREAM MAY FORETELL AN OUTER MEETING OF SIGNIFICANCE.

Many people have reported dreams which predicted a relationship or other event in their life. The sceptics can always pick apart any statement based on the imperfection inherent in understanding any experience. Yet in viewing the authenticity of a report we consider the person and the overall direction of the evidence. For the example in this section the author will use his own experience. Normally he is not given to the esoteric, or portraying imaginative encounters as concretely real. The following is what happened to him. Many people probably could have similar experiences if they practised inner awareness.

Example: On a railway trip back to a conference on dreams the author dreamed he was in a class given by a dark-haired woman who was vital, alive, and attractive. After the class he went up to her and they both felt this electric energy between them. He said to himself in the dream, this is a woman I can marry. The next day at the conference he met such a woman and they established a powerful relationship which might have led to marriage had not outside circumstances, including living 1000 miles away from each other, intervened. (Predictive dream in that the event of a deep mutual attraction is a rare event. How could the Dream Source know ahead of the ego?)

Comment: The author was not looking for a relationship at the conference, yet the dream did shock him when he woke. He had taken the dream as an inner experience and had not sought to act it out at the conference. Then meeting such a dynamic woman opened his heart in a deep way. They were immediately attracted. The rest is history.

In following this and other Relationship Dreams we note the power of relationship, inner and outer. Relating to an outer partner can evoke tremendous forces within. The author has had other significant relationships, yet it has been mainly with the 'dream enhanced' women he has felt the deeper *soulmate* quality, a tremendous catalysing of forces. It is as if *destiny* is that which happens as powerfully in the outer as it does in the inner.

Issue: What if lovers or married people have not dreamed of each other with major intensity? Often one partner will dream more about the other partner. The one who has the partner in the dream is the more evoked one. The ideal relationship may be one in which both partners are equally evoked by the other. They dream of each other and both together. This suggests the potential for relationship has quickened them to the core. With partners who hardly dream of each other we can only suggest their lives together are too settled and need a shaking up. Or is it they have been integrating well what is being evoked between them and do not need to dream process their relationship?

If you want to find out how deeply your love with another moves you, look to your dreams. You will see there what a partner evokes for you and the potential destiny you can choose to achieve together.

43. RELATING TO PEOPLE WE KNOW IN OUR DREAMS MAY INVOLVE DEALING WITH PROBLEMS AND OPPORTUNITIES IN THE OUTER LIFE RELATIONSHIPS

Apparently the Dream Source is there to help us with our relationships. What point of view does the Dream Source take? The Dream Source presents us with our pattern in the relationship and thereby gives us insight and choice in how we can relate to the outer person.

Example: A man dreams his wife is sitting on one bench and he on the other. A fish leaps over the sand and swims around the walls of the room. He pulls out a knife to pin it to the wall yet realises that would kill the fish. Does he want to do that? He wakes up with this issue. (Ego Issues dream with the Dream Source presenting new consciousness and issues to the dreamer.)

Comment: From this dramatic dream the dreamer realises his tendency to try to pin everything down in the relationship. He recognises this as one of his major issues causing difficulty and decides in the dream not to pin the fish down. Better to flow with and relate to things as they are in the relationship. The dream becomes a teaching parable for the dreamer, and indeed for all of us. From now on his wife will have an easier time in relating to him since she will have more freedom in expressing herself without worry that her partner is going to pin her down to some behaviour or statement as if it were a truth or obligation for all time. They both have been working hard in couple's counselling, making this also a Confirming dream.

Relationships are best handled with a sense of flow and yielding to each situation as it comes up rather than trying to fit into categories and commitments what is essentially a feeling and at times irrational process.

44. RELATING IN DREAMS TO PEOPLE WE KNOW IN THE OUTER MAY INVOLVE DEALING WITH WHAT THEY EVOKE IN US, OUR PROJECTIONS ON TO THEM, OR THEIRS UPON US.

We are in relationship with another to be able to find ourselves better. In a conscious relationship we may learn more about ourselves than about the person we are relating to. A *conscious relationship* is one in which

65

one or both parties are actively making known to themselves and each other the dynamics in them evoked by the relationship. They are also integrating what becomes known so the relationship does not become burdened by unconscious energy. *The compulsive need to know the other person is the need to know ourselves better.*

Example: A woman dreamed that before an actual meeting with her lover she would go to the rendezvous with a list of demands for him to conform to. She took the dream to heart and looked at her tendency to meet her insecurity needs by putting demands on the other person. Her lover was not the kind of man who responded to a woman's demands. (Ego Issues dream preparing the dreamer for a realistic relationship encounter.)

Comment: The rendezvous turned out better than expected. There were indeed difficulties between them which she could do nothing about. Yet her openness allowed them to be close despite the issues and she left feeling good about how well she had handled his and her feelings. She recognised the demands she wanted to make were her inner longings for a relationship easier than the present one. She also understood more what she would look for if and when they ended their relationship.

We cannot demand a relationship be a certain way. We can process our longing by contrasting what the reality of the present relationship is with what we would like to have if we had a new relationship.

Longing for a new relationship can mean we have learned what there is to learn from the present one and it is time to move on to a more evocative and deeper relationship. Experiencing longing also can mean we are not doing the inner work of developing in ourselves what we miss out there in the other person.

45. RELATING TO OUTER LIFE PEOPLE IN DREAMS MAY INVOLVE OUR PSYCHIC ATTUNEMENT WITH HIDDEN PARTS OF OUR PARTNERS OR THEIR LIVES.

Of course at some level we know what our intimate partner is doing or feeling whether they tell us or not, yet we may not let ourselves see the truth unless we operate from intuition and face our insecurities.

Example: A woman dreamed her boyfriend brought a new woman to his apartment and made love to her. The next day she called him and reported the dream, asking him if it were true. He said, yes. (Intuition dream showing the actual relationship situation and possibly actual outer events.)

Comment: This couple was in the midst of deciding whether to end their relationship. Obviously one of the pair was making his own choice by taking up with another woman. Not to be left behind, the dreamer's source let her be instantly in tune with the situation so she could know what she was dealing with. She acted promptly, went over, they had their talk and tears, and ended their relationship.

Ending a relationship in a healing way requires intunement with what is. It requires honesty to face the facts, and open communication to give each a sense of reality and the ability to move on in life with little left hanging.

46. DREAM RELATING MAY INVOLVE MALE–FEMALE DYNAMICS.

Males and females are distinguished from each other by their genitals. Basic root energies of the universe differentiate the sexes. The male erect *penis* is a thrusting tool symbolising the assertive and catalytic energy of life. The female moist *vagina* is the receiving vessel symbolising that energy which opens and receives life. *Masculine* archetypal energy is *intentional*. *Feminine* archetypal energy is *receptive*. Both sexes have both dynamics within their psyches, yet biology usually determines which one is predominent.

The Feminine and Masculine Archetypes

Figure 5 shows how the *masculine* and *feminine* operate together through the *Self Centre*. A key idea is that men and women are differentiated sexually not just for the biological urge to produce babies and relationship but also to embody for each other opposite archetypal energies inherent in the universe. This explains the tremendous attraction between the sexes which goes beyond sex as simply an instinctual experience. We have within us, regardless of sex, both masculine and feminine dynamics. The man most often identifies with his male genitals and their corresponding archetypal functions of *assertion, structure,* and *doing* among others. The woman most often identifies with her female genitals and their archetypal functions of *receiving, nurturing,* and *being*. Each sex then projects the opposite archetypal characteristics onto the biological opposites who embody them most closely. When two people are projected out onto each other in this way they usually seek to unite physically and psychologically to have the unity experience of the *Self Centre*, expressed in sexual orgasm. Here *biology replicates psychology*. The energy dynamics in the universe and in the psyche are the motivating forces for producing unity and new life.

In dreams we also see these archetypal forces, thus explaining in part why we often have more variety of sexual expression in our dreams than in outer life. Social mores and other things inhibit the full archetypal demonstration, so we must also find fulfilment in our dreams.

Example: In her dream a woman is making love with a woman yogi who has a beautiful genital. The dreamer starts making love to her and their body parts are entwined, not knowing what goes where. The yogi also has two penises, one on each thigh. Everything is intermingled. It is quite an experience. (Archetypal dream in which issues of archetypal energies are most important for the dreamer's consciousness and choice-making.)

Comment: This dreamer was dealing with an outer relational issue of being attracted to aggressive men who were not good for her and not being attracted to sensitive men who liked her. The Dream Source could be showing her a state of confusion as well as the next step in development. She is attracted to men identified with the male organ and not to their female energy which she herself has in abundance. So being feminine she seeks mates who are her opposite. However, she needs to develop more inner masculine which will make her less attracted to macho men. She can raise her sexual level to a more integrative stage and work on relating to men who have some of their feminine developed. In the dream she is relating to a feminine woman who also has the masculine principle. Perhaps the dreamer should have one of the two penises? And in the act of sex she does, not knowing what is hers and what isn't in her sensual merger.

Sex is not sex. It is the expression of primary energies between people and within oneself.

47. WE CAN DISCOVER THE TRUE NATURE OF OUR SEXUAL EXPRESSION THROUGH OUR DREAMS.

If sex is not sex, what then is it? We participate in sex with various people throughout our lives, and at one level we are having sexual experience, a physiological experience of great release and pleasure. Yet at another deeper level our sexual activity is an expression of unconscious patterns deep within us created in childhood, and influenced by cultural attitudes. Dreams can show us the underlying patterns governing our sexual behaviour. (See Chapter 6, Objectifying Dreams and Researching Dreams for how to find the patterns.)

Example: In this dream a couple in relationship are bored with each other. The dreamer says that does not have to be and she will help them. All of them get naked and make love together. The dreamer is lying on top of the woman and brings her to orgasm while the man penetrates the dreamer from behind yet she does not have an orgasm. The couple never really touch. The dreamer goes down the hallway to masturbate, yet people interrupt her. Finally an ex-boyfriend comes along and takes her somewhere. (Ego Issues dream in which the ego tries to make archetypal expression happen which is not happening.)

Comment: The dreamer is participating in a threesome. She is engaging in sex to make others happy and is left with the issue, what about pleasing herself? She is having sex, yet what good is it doing her? She is between the couple. They do not make direct sexual contact. Then she masturbates to make contact with herself. Yet even here the contact is broken. What then is the purpose of sex so far in this dream? What seems to be developing is that the dreamer uses sex to help others. She has learned to 'service' others sexually, yet since she is not in contact with herself she is not in contact with others. Blocks and wrong choices stand in the way of achieving a deep and relational contact with another as well as with herself. The 'sexual bridge' is broken and the sex does not work. Archetypal expression cannot be dictated by the ego, and only occurs when the conditions are right, creating a fulfilling experience.

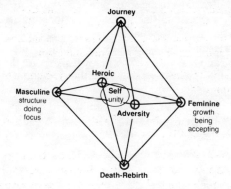

Figure 5   Masculine and Feminine Archetypes showing that they are opposites interacting through the unity function of the Central Archetype of the Self.

48. DREAMS BRING OUT THE REAL ISSUES IN A RELATIONSHIP.

People often think they know what their problems are in a relationship. Yet this is the ego speaking. We have a conscious view of ourselves and our partners yet this is often a mask hiding what is happening underneath. The real truth is that many people learn to hide themselves in intimate relationships. They find out soon enough that to reveal their full vulnerability will make them liable to hurt from their partners. So in effect *we build strong defence systems to survive intimate relating*. This causes *repression* and *evasion*, making intimate and open relating difficult. Dreamwork reveals the real issues beneath the layer of repression, and when revealed, all hell breaks loose in a marriage. And why not? Should a primary relationship become a prison for love or a revealer? It is not simple to love. *Love means revealing the wounds as well as their salvation.*

Example: In the dream the dreamer's wife tells him she is not attracted to him any more yet she wants them to stay together for appearances. The dreamer responds, 'No way! If that's the case I want out of this relationship right now.' She replies, 'Well, if that's how you feel, maybe we can develop a different kind of relationship, even move to the country.' (Ego Issues dream revealing relational issues and how the dreamer wants to deal with them.)

Comment: What are the problems here? The wife does not want intimacy? The dreamer does not want a relationship of appearances only? The real issue may not be the specific content but how they relate. When she puts forth a position he puts forth his counter-position, and then she changes her previous position. Through it all they have one basic commitment, and that is to having a relationship. How each of them defines what they want in the relationship seems to differ. This issue certainly is at the core of their outer relationship. They are close and real with each other, yet also want things the other person is not able or willing to give. It hardly seems probable that what is depicted here is only the dreamer's inner workings. Instead, the Dream Source presents a perspective on how the couple are relating in the outer, and what to do with this situation. This they work on in couple's counselling, using their dreams to work on the inner to be able to make the outer changes necessary.

49. DREAMS MAY SYMBOLISE THE NATURE OF THE RELATIONAL BOND.

Quite literally, the *wedding ring* becomes itself a symbol for the relationship, as in the following examples.

Example: A husband who did know his wife was secretly planning to leave him, dreamed he had lost his wedding ring. He woke and told her the dream. Soon she told him she was leaving. (Intuition dream revealing the true state of the relationship.)

Example: A wife dreamed she looked down at her wedding ring and saw the diamond was missing. (Ego Issues Dream revealing unconsciousness around a relationship commitment.)

Comment: In outer life the couple in the second example had never been able to decide on buying a wedding ring. She used her grandmother's ring yet had stopped wearing it. This indicates a hidden flaw or reservation about being fully married. Many times these days the man will not even wear a wedding ring, often indicating a lack of full commitment or willingness to be bounded in by love.

50. IN DREAMS WE CAN EXPERIENCE THE DARK SIDE AS WELL AS THE BRIGHT SIDE OF RELATIONSHIP.

The *dark side* usually refers to *sex* and *violence*. The *shadow* is the repository within us of that which we keep under cover from the world. Some of the most vital aspects of intimate relating are done in private. For intimate relationship is itself an arena wherein the shadow is especially prominent.

Example: A young woman dreamed she and her boyfriend started making love in a room where other could see what they were doing. They had both taken off their trousers and had their genitals united. At first she tried to keep that part of themselves covered with a large pillow, but then in the heat of their passion the pillow fell away. (Ego Issues Dream highlighting attitudes around the free expression of sexuality.)

Comment: The dreamer was hesitant and embarrassed to share her sex dream. The dream group was understanding and alert. For sex itself holds a tremendous energy for many people and therefore has a whole body of attitudes and values surrounding it. Yet why was the Dream Source presenting her and her boyfriend in such a compromising position? One of the effects of her sharing this dream was to better

THE ELEMENTS OF DREAMWORK

accept her sexuality. The healthy attitude would be more, *I make love intensely and enjoy the activity. It aids my health and well-being and enhances my relationship.* Thus the dream presents the dark side of the person and the relationship. Their love-making was done in semi-public and not in private. Too much privacy can be inhibitory to the life process. Expressing oneself openly demands tremendous self-acceptance. Obviously her parents did not practice their sexuality semi-openly as the children were growing up.

51. THROUGH DREAMS AND DREAMWORK WE CAN CONTINUE RELATING TO THE SPIRITS OF THE DEAD TO RESOLVE THE RELATIONSHIP WITHIN OURSELVES.

Example: A woman in her twenties had a dream in which her father, who had been killed in a war when she was thirteen, visited her. In her dreamwork she re-entered the dream and told him how her life as a young woman had gone since his death. She was in tears throughout the whole process, and felt a sense of relief and deep acceptance after. (Expression dream making possible a relating which could not happen in outer life, thus giving an experience of fulfilment where previously there has been loss.)

Comment: Was she communing with the spirit essence of her dead father, or simply with a father dynamic inside herself representing parental acceptance? Can we ever know? What is central to this process is at a feeling level she treated the dream as a real experience, as real as outer life experiences yet different. The results were positive for her emotional health. That is what is central. If the spirits of the dead exist in ways outside our rational knowing, contact through the dream world may be an important avenue and a deeply felt spiritual experience.

Example: When a psychiatrist colleague of the author died of a mysterious brain tumour which the doctors diagnosed yet never found in the autopsy, the author wrote him a goodbye letter. In the letter the author mildly chided the psychiatrist for never expressing his anger or even saying he had any. The author awoke with a dream in which the psychiatrist was standing at the foot of the bed with a slight reproving frown on his face. (Expression dream using dreams as an arena for expressing feelings no longer possible to express in the outer and receiving confirmation of their value. Possibly Psychic Communication dream also, but who knows?)

Comment: The author in his 'spirit letter' acknowledged the nature of their relationship, the positive and negative, and then in the night received a dream of relationship. The psychiatrist came and expressed some anger, completing the wholeness picture for himself and the author. It was a moving and deeply felt experience for at least one of them.

SUMMARY

Dreamwork is an excellent vehicle not only for learning about oneself but also for learning about relationships. We see in our dreams how we relate and do not relate to others. We do dreamwork with our dreams by taking how we act, or need to act in dreams, into outer relationships. *We learn about the outer by going inner.* Dreams may show our difficulties in relating, as well as the actuality of our sexual lives. We learn about our defensiveness in relating and how past experiences influence us. We find out about male-female dynamics. We can have fulfilling relational experiences in dreams when they may not be happening in our outer lives. We can know through our dreams what our intimate partners are doing, whether they tell us or not. Following the dream and its revelations creates more honest and realistic relating, and contributes to resolving relationships which are about to be over. This leads to ending major relationships as well as beginning new ones. Such work can also help us to transform a present relationship into a deeper one, a soul journey in which both of a couple are actively working on themselves and the relationship. We may even have relational contact with the spirits of the dead through our dreams. Primary dreamwork techniques to use with relationship dreams are Following the Dream Ego, Rewriting the Dream, Dialogueing with Dream Figures, and Dream Re-entry.

THINGS TO DO

- Take a number of your dreams in which a relational partner or family member appears and list how you relate or do not relate to that person. Do not make a judgment about that other person but describe instead your relational pattern regarding her or him. Then devise creative changes you would like to make in the outer relationship, do these changes and see how the results are reflected in new dreams.

- Look closely at recent dreams to research and describe your defence system as it shows up in dreams and relationships. Do you hide? Get angry? Try to dominate? Criticise? Act elusive? Then describe more creative and direct ways of relating which you can begin in outer life and which you may be doing once in a while in dream life.

- Look at the strangers in your dreams. How do they express themselves? What of their expressiveness can you also take on yourself? In dreams? In outer life?

- Describe and share some examples of your first seeing the potential for the future in the dream state. How active were you in carrying out this potential?

- List the problems and opportunities you are having in your relationship based on how these show up in your recent dreams. What are you doing about them in relationship?

- What projections on to partners, positive and negative, need consciousness and integration based on what your dreams are showing you?

- What are some of the unspoken things you suspect or know about others which seem to be showing up in your dreams? Commit yourself to checking these intuitions out with those involved so you can see if they are outward perceptions or inner perceptions needing new consciousness.

- What are your dreams saying about your sexual and aggressive life? List in detail and then apply to actual outer relating.

- Devise ways of sharing your relational dreams with those involved, and they with you, so you may increase the intimacy between you. Be cautious if you both are not being real with each other, and are therefore not processing together your relationship issues. And why then are you in such an unreal relationship if you are not sharing consciously and with caring?

- With someone you have been close to who has died look to continuing the relationship in future dreaming. At a feeling level this is real and leads to new relatedness and fulfilment.

- Finally, when you have a relationship dream, review the above questions and apply the relevant ones to your dream.

5 · Dreams and Healing

What we do not deal with in life will come up in our dreams. Dreams do not scare us to keep us frightened, but to motivate us to deal with that which we would reject.

A woman dreamed there was a large crocodile in the water and, though he looked ferocious, she knew her task was to face the animal in all its being and to accept it for what it is.

The man left the house where the people were, crossed a creek, and climbed to the top of a ledge where a sliver of cliff jutted straight out. He slid himself onto the ledge and lay there flat on his back looking up. Presently he heard the rock ledge crack and said to himself, here it goes. He did not feel afraid or try to wake himself because he was going to die. He let himself fall with the rock, knowing he was probably falling to his death. The ledge hit the water forty feet below and bounced ashore. He had survived! But greater yet, he had at last gone with the experience instead of resisting it. In a series of childhood dreams he would start across a bridge and a hole would open up, causing him to fall through. He always woke before the fall completed itself. Later he learned to fly in his dreams yet never once went back to a bridge scene. (Confirming Dream and also a Great Dream because it illustrates a real breakthrough this dreamworker is making in his psyche and life.)

Thus we begin a major chapter of this book. The dreamworker has been working with his dreams and his life for almost a year and going through profound changes. He is at last tackling his anxiety and coping with adversarial situations through acceptance, presence, choice, and finally healing. He has learned that to be healed he must first go through the conflict, grounding anxiety in present fear, and choosing how he will relate to the situation. He does not try to control things, or even resist them. Nor does he try to dominate the situation by defeating adversity. He brings consciousness, and the commitment to work things through no matter the cost, no matter how imperfectly he accomplishes his task. He has become a Dream Warrior in the primary sense of the image. Life will never be the same. He will still always have much to deal with, yet now his attitude and his heart is different. He can feel again, go through Death-Rebirth into new life. The Dream Warrior is now also the Spiritual Warrior who takes this world as it is and creates with it. Now is the time of his present moment, his birth into life.

Comment: By letting go of control and allowing the dream to go to resolution, even if it meant his own death, this dreamer is transforming a potentially negative experience into a positive one. *Fear of falling is fear of letting go of control of life.* Many people resist their scary dreams. They wake themselves before the terrible can happen. Yet this dreamer finally faced up to the fact that he was afraid and went through it. The paradox is that what we fear is annihilation and how to get over the fear is to risk annihilation. *You go through the fear to get to the healing.*

This is not *lucid dreaming* (dream control). The dreamer is *not* telling himself in the dream, 'this is only a dream and it won't hurt me to fall'. He is participating in the dream as real, as risky, as dealing with fear by going through what he is afraid of. He is having a Great Dream. To do this he must believe his dreams are real and sometimes dangerous. He must have authentic feeling experiences of them. The results in this person's life were amazing. He learned to deal with fear at all sorts of levels and make valuable life choices he was not capable of before. He was also a business manager supervising many people, and naturally enough, dreamwork affected his waking work as well as his intimate relationships. He has earned the right to be visited with a Great Dream by dealing with his other dreams of being afraid. A *Great Dream* is a dream that is an authentic experience of being real, and in which the crisis is resolved through creative dream ego activity in alliance with the deeper centre, the Dream Source.

52. HEALING IS THE PROCESS OF BRINGING RESOLUTION TO OPPOSITIONS IN THE PSYCHE, THE BODY, AND LIFE.

All we can ask of ourselves is that we face reality as it is, not as we would want it to be. Too often we are in opposition with life and each other because we keep ourselves stuck in a *problem*, an irreconcilable condition with as yet little commitment to its transformation into wholeness. How we deal with adversarial dreams makes very clear our approach to ourselves and life. Are we committed to healing in ourselves, in situations, in others, no matter what sacrifices it takes? How many of us can answer Yes to this? I personally am committed to this principle and practice, yet at times I barely seem to survive it. Yet when the results come in, and they are meaningful, it makes the whole process worth the effort.

What healing is not

It is usually not healing to run from adversaries in dreams or in life. Some people forget their bad or horrific dreams. Do you? They also ignore their Skunk Dreams, the ones where the toilet is overflowing with shit, or they are being violent or sexually outrageous. An interesting issue is raised here.

Do the same rules of outer life apply in dream life? This is the question of the *shadow*, the repressed and underdeveloped part of ourselves. When you are being sexual with your neighbour's wife or husband in your dream are you violating your actual outer marriage?

Do the same constraints apply to inner life as they do to outer? In this approach to dreamwork we recognise we are the same person inner and outer. We are one whole although the actual dreams show us as split personalities until we are well on our way in a committed dreamwork process.

If we practise repression of certain issues, feelings, and emotions in outer life, these same repressions will show up in dreams as the adversaries which plague us. What we avoid dealing with in outer life will be brought up again by the Dream Source to deal with on the inner level. The dream is the more whole view of us since it includes the dark side as well as our positive characteristics, and even our greatest moments.

Dreamwork is the middle arena between inner and outer. With this as our choice the same constraints we try to live under in the outer do not apply to the dream state. Yes, it may be important in a dream to kill an adversary rather than always be threatened by them. Or to love your neighbour's wife, a young boy, your father, your mother, someone awful, someone beautiful, someone unknown, someone quite familiar. If it happens, experience it fully rather than cut off from these demon acts because you do not admit them into your *persona*, the good side of yourself. The real danger is we will also repress our inner life activity, as we might constrain ourselves in the outer. Then the energy has nowhere to express itself for release, transformation and integration. *Through dreamwork we can more fully experience the dark side of life than we can in outer life with its societal and ethical restraints.*

No, your dreams of darkness, chaos, and great difficulty do not necessarily show you are neurotic, criminal, or psychotic. They show that which you need to deal with for increased wholeness. The advanced people in the work may suffer more problems and difficulties than the average person trying to live an average normal life. Nor is it healthy and whole to strive for spiritual enlightenment without demons and adversaries whose function might well be to keep you grounded.

Healing is not ignoring ordinary dreams in favour of cosmic dreams, or seeing only the good parts of dreams, or changing your nasty dream encounters into positive encounters with the fight and the fear and the fucking taken out of them. It cannot be healing for the ego to attempt still to dominate the dream and life, for in order to control we try to exclude that which threatens our control. The ego calls the good that which it can master to meet its needs. *Our demons are all those things which we cannot control.* Until we face them and accept them we shall continue our losing battles with fate. *There is no final alternative but to face what we most fear.*

What in life is not healing

What we do not deal with in life will come up in our dreams. No wonder many of us seek to forget our dreams. What is not healing in life is trying to get more sleep than we need as a way of avoiding the realities of outer life. What is not healing is experiencing anger yet not owning its effect on ourselves and others. What is not healing is not dealing with the adversarial nature of life, of not practising centring in everything we do, not accepting reality exactly as it is, living in fantasies without making choices to transform and actualise them. *What is not healing is trying to make an ideal dream out of life.*

53. WE COMMIT TO DEALING WITH DREAM AND OUTER LIFE ADVERSARIES FOR HEALING AND NEW LIFE.

Dream adversaries are any figures or situations which seem opposing or destroying. *Nightmares* are adversarial dreams. A nightmare is any dream that makes us wake ourselves up out of fear. In these dreams we are typically opposed and attacked. These attacks and assertions often create fear in the dream ego, which runs away or ultimately escapes from the situation by waking up. In order to escape the adversary in the nightmare we wake ourselves into waking reality.

What happens when the going gets tough in outer reality? We try to wake up from dream reality, next we try to make ourselves unconscious by falling asleep when we are in fear. In both instances we create an attempt at escape in fear of adversarial forces. Why do we have nightmares or fear dreams? Because we are trying to escape that which would oppose or destroy our attempts at control.

We can learn how to deal with that side of life which is destructive. *Many people have been taught to flee from dangerous forces rather than face them.* Running away may be a temporary expedient yet it excludes half of life. A major step is to deal effectively with adversarial forces, not by fleeing them but by coping with them directly. *Better to stay present in adversity than to have it destroy us through our flight.*

Example: I dreamed the earth was trembling underneath me and I decided to fly away. As I was leaping from the ground to fly the earth opened and a fanatic came out and gave me three fatal karate chops which killed me. I switched into the observer when this happened. (Compensatory dream to conscious attitude of being able to handle things through escape.)

Comment: We carefully note in this dream an earthquake did not happen. The ground trembled and the dream ego was afraid it would occur and tried to flee the scene. This did not work because a greater adversary rose up and killed her. What she most feared happened to her! *We deal with nightmares by facing the adversaries, not fleeing from them, just as in life. It is better to face adversity than flee from it.* Yet then we would have to give up control and simply stay present with what is happening.

In the American Senoi Dreamwork Tradition dreamers are trained to stop running and to start relating in their dreams. When we flee from something we give it our energy in addition to its own. If however, we turn and face our enemy the enemy might turn into a friend. *We are most afraid of what we have not yet integrated within ourselves.*

Fear is itself the perception of possible loss. We are afraid our possessions will be stolen, our lovers and spouses will be taken from us, our limbs will go in accidents, our money will disappear in a financial crisis, our children will end up a disaster because we are not there to save them, and that our lives will be taken away from us before our time. Interestingly enough, at the fear level none of the above are actual and therefore something to immediately deal with. As events they do happen all the time. The Adversarial Archetype is a major force throughout all existence for all time. Yet mostly our experience of fear is of *possible*, not *actual* loss.

We fear the possible, not the actual. We are afraid of what could happen, of events which have not yet happened! Why waste a moment on what does not exist?

One cure for fear is to keep yourself in the moment and not wander off into the potentials of the future. Certainly we may take measures to deal with possible catastrophe, yet to dwell in the future and try to control it from the present is sheer folly. Our best approach is to stay fully in the present and deal with things as they arise.

People untrained in adversarial work react to fear with avoidance.

You feel pain and you withdraw. Humans feel also the *possibility of pain*. They don't even wait for the real pain. This may be why so many people wake themselves up in a nightmare instead of going through it. And why lucid dreamers try to control their dreams and change adversarial energy rather than go through the test of facing a challenge.

Dreamwork with Adversarial dreams can train you to deal creatively with adversity in life. Don't expect life to be good and beautiful. Expect it to be real and exclude nothing from your encounter.

Some typical adversarial dream scenes

Examples: I dreamed a huge wave was coming and was about to overwhelm me. I dreamed a snake was about to bite me and I woke up. I dreamed I was supposed to be somewhere important and I could not find the place. I dreamed something came up behind me and choked me. I struggled and woke. I dreamed a dark figure was after me and I could not get away even though I kept running. I dreamed I had murdered somebody and the police were after me. I dreamed the atomic bomb was about to go off and it was the end for all of us. I dreamed I was falling and woke afraid. An animal was about to get me. I realised it was a dream and made myself fly out of its reach. (Each of these dreams can be seen as both Compensatory and Amplifying, in that they compensate for the conscious attitude of being in control and amplify the underlying insecurity and fear that one is not actually in control of oneself or life. We also could simply call them Adversarial dreams.)

These dreams are *unresolved*. The principle and practise of resolving all dreams has not been applied here. In each dream the dream ego is *under challenge to give up control*. The dreamer has not learned to apply a different principle than control to dealing with adversarial energy. When the dreamer cannot control the force of the dream then the ego uses *flight* as its response. The dreamer has not yet trained him or herself in controlling flight and maintaining presence.

Why are dream events often more horrific than outer events in a person's life? In working through nightmares as process work we often reach a level in which past real traumas such as abuse, accident, loss, and betrayal surface with all the original repressed emotions now being acted out in fits of anger, numbness, crying, and pure anguish. Thus the contemporary dangers in dreams and in life are amplified by repressed material from the past. In working with the dream we work with that which the dream reflects, the blocked emotional energy in the psyche.

Or as one person remarked, she is not having nightmares because her outer life is nightmarish. The other great danger is taking refuge in a 'beautiful' dream life which compensates the external situation. The corrective is to actualise the dream potentials in external life, and to deal with the outer adversities by using our dreamwork principles of staying present and balancing the energy in the 'outer dream' as well as the inner dream.

54. RECEIVING THE DREAM ADVERSARY IS NECESSARY TO WHOLENESS.

In the actualisation approach dreamers relive their dreams as valid emotional experiences. If they have not remembered or achieved the feeling level in telling their dream then through dreamwork techniques such as Dream Re-entry and Dream Enactment, dreamers are enabled to feel the full effect of the dream. This allows the person to experience dream situations in as real a way as outer life situations.

The experience of *wholeness* is when all aspects of ourselves are functioning in related ways. Excluding adversarial dynamics causes splits in the psyche. Including adversarial dynamics within the total allows the wholeness pattern to resolve in a new and integrative way.

Wholeness and healing can come only with inclusion and then resolution. Dreams do not scare us to keep us frightened, but to motivate us to deal with that which we would reject.

81

Example: A woman dreamed there was a large crocodile in the water and, though he looked ferocious, she knew her task was to face the animal in all its being and to accept it for what it is. (Teaching dream in that it gives the dreamer basic life wisdom, it teaches.)

Comment: Her own comment was this meant accepting her basic instinctual nature. She never explained what that was specifically since she was not in a dream group. Yet we can imagine all sorts of instinctual behaviour which could be seen as devouring. New forms of sexual expression. Having sex outside your marriage. Getting angry at your spouse. Getting out of your rational arguments into a feeling impulsive kind of responding. Who knows? It will differ for different people. The suggestion was she *dialogue* with the crocodile to see what he wanted from her. Her attitude was right, and her potential adversary powerful. In fact nothing terrible happened in the dream. It is so easy to project our fears of what might happen on to what is actually happening. *If you accept situations just as you see them, and don't project into them, then you will be able to deal with all aspects of life as they come up.* So there is wisdom in meeting the crocodile of your dreams!

Repression and avoidance cause us to live only half of life. Not only does it take energy to repress energy. We also miss out on so much life through fear and avoidance. To commit to wholeness as a process means *to go where the fear is.* One of our ongoing tasks can be to continually enlarge the circle of what we shall encompass in life. All Adversarial dreams seem to be asking this of us, so dreamwork is a good place to practise. We leap into life *living at the edge of risk!* Is there any other way?

55. RELATING CREATIVELY TO DREAM ADVERSARIES TRAINS ONE IN HANDLING OUTER LIFE ADVERSARIES AS WELL

Example: A dreamer dreamed a large woman in white was about to inject him with a long hypodermic needle, and he woke feeling very afraid. (Compensatory dream in that it presents the opposite to the dreamer's over-controlling attitude and behaviour.)

Comment: This is a similar theme to the dream bite. It is still 'an intervention of the Other', an issue of response to being controlled, or controlling. Through dreamwork we can learn how to go through being controlled and cope with it in other ways than contraction or flight. Receive the injection and see what happens? Is this the needed reaction to this dream? What other dreamwork approach would actually help dreamers allow adversity in?

Dreamwork example: In the Guided Re-entry a tall woman in white like a nurse's uniform was coming towards the dreamer again with a long hypodermic needle. He was asked just to let the scene stop there and feel the tension. What were his alternatives? He said he could try to grab the hypodermic, throw the woman across the room, or let her stick the needle into him. These alternatives were quite real to the dreamer, as he was panting hard. He chose to receive the needle. It went into his arm and stuck there. He was surprised it did not hurt and that it would not come out. This meant the woman was also stuck to him and he started waving her about in the air trying to get rid of her. She turned into a black witch as he kept flinging her about. This was his impasse. Neither of them would change. The next suggestion was he relax his energy and let go completely. The witch became a heap of rags at his feet. Shudders of energy went through his body as he lay out flat on his stomach feeling the relief. To end the re-entry he was guided back into a sitting position and for re-grounding him in his body, the sitting position being half way into consciousness again.

Comment: These dramatic results are realised because the dreamer courageously chose to stay present to adversarial energy, receive it, and deal with it. The last thing in the world most people are trained to do is receive adversarial energy. Therefore they block, become frightened, and compound an adversarial situation with resistance. After his feeling experience in the body, this dreamer was also able to stay present better with his wife when she was doing feeling things which might bewilder him and which he chose no longer to try to control. He did not have to see her as adversary any more just because she did things differently.

Fallacy: Many people have the view that the desirable psychological state is to be healthy, happy, and positive about life. This attitude does not equip them for dealing with adversarial forces in life and in dreams because then they want to avoid the rough stuff of life instead of welcoming it.

Alternative: Adopting a new attitude or principle, the wholeness principle, will enable people to adapt to and cope with adversarial energy.

56. WITHIN OURSELVES AND ALL OF LIFE ARE TWO GREAT OPPOSITE AND STRUGGLING ENERGIES: HEROIC VERSUS ADVERSITY

We look again at our model of the archetypes to see how two other great primary energies work in ourselves, in life, and in our dreams. An *archetype* is a primary energy of existence. Whether we like it or not, these energies are the cosmos's basic units. Almost all people prefer the Heroic Archetype, that which saves, is good, is successful, is positive. The ego, for some reason, has a bias towards the positive. It prefers pleasure over pain, goodness over bad, healing over sickness. This bias is unrealistic simply because in life there exist the opposites. For all humankind's longing for peace there has always been violence and bloodshed, and now we have the threat of nuclear holocaust restraining us as a world from all out war. The destructive impulse will have to be expressed in other ways, including dreamwork and martial arts, another arena, one among many. It can no longer be argued that war, that evil itself, is simply the absence of good, and that if we were only perfect enough we would be peaceful and kindly towards each other and never have bad thoughts, dreams, or actions. Now we are being asked to include the Destroyer, even evil, within our commitment to wholeness. Certainly this shows up in dreams, as when we have committed some dream crime and are hiding from the authorities.

We do not keep evil out. We integrate it within the very heart of our being so it may transform and be transformed in the encounter with its opposite, the good, the beautiful, the healthy side of life. Wholeness

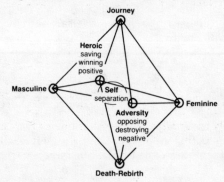

Figure 6   The Seven Basic Archetypes model emphasising the relation of the Heroic Archetype to that of Adversity.

means including the dark side, the imperfect and even destructive aspect of life in all we do.

Evil is used here as another word for the destructive force in the universe, that which kills, maims, opposes, destroys. Another aspect of evil would be the conscious choice by an individual to identify with the Adversarial Archetype. 'Moral evil' involves choice. We can choose to destroy where necessary, yet to consciously identify with destruction is morally evil, which itself destroys a person's soul, the ability to live a meaningful life. However, people who consciously identify with Heroic or positive energy, the good people, are also not moral people in this sense.

Yes, the moral person is one who can consciously choose between good and evil, sometimes doing the one and sometimes the other, both within a context of meaning.

The psychologist, Fritz Kunkle, once told how when he came to America and had a number of Quakers in analysis, their dreams were full of violence, although on the outside they professed to be Friends and pacifists.

A person identified with only the good and the light in life does not have choice since they are taken over by one opposite. Identification with the good also tends to create evil as a reaction to one-sidedness. In our dream examples you will see dreamers accepting and coping with the dark side rather than any longer rejecting it, fleeing from it, identifying with it, or making it good. Encountering and expressing 'evil' does not mean we act out whatever energy is evoked in us. Yet we do encounter it and make it relevant to our lives. We create with the destructive force of life as well as the creative.

A major human fallacy

We have the fundamental assumption that the way to deal with adversarial energy is to resist it. Either we oppose violence with violence or we try to flee from or exclude it as the 'good' Christian might. Such approaches increase violence on both sides and can evoke war, leading to destruction of both adversaries and a resolution which can only occur with the defeat of one or both parties. Most games are played in this win-lose format, as if instinctively the cultures of the world must still train their youth in the ancient art of war.

The new way

Blend with adversarial energy rather than resist it, create with it, include it within a larger whole. Our goal is to bring adversarial energy within a larger pattern of wholeness wherein it can serve its part yet not be a cancer to the whole. Resisting evil makes it want to come in. Invite evil in and you accept the destroying force within the schema of your own existence. Exclude it and it will get all of you. *What we most fear is what we will become.* Include it and it will only be a part of the whole.

Remember one of the goals of dreamwork is for the dream ego to take on more and more the energy and character of other dream figures.

Example: On the author's birthday he had a dream in which he and his ex-wife were captured by Samurai. They were made to stand for a long time. She went crazy and was taken away. He endured and finally the Samurai master came and said he should have bowed immediately when he was captured. The author did this now. The master took a Japanese fine sword from his assistant, tore apart the wrappings and handed it to the author, who felt a profound reverence for what had just happened with the sword and knew he would be in training with this master for the rest of his life. (Revelatory or Teaching dream in that it presents a major new step in life, therefore also a Great dream.)

Comment: Here we see the blending with the adversary. It did no good resisting the situation in the least or trying to win. Bowing down to those who have power over you acknowledges that power and your willingness not to resist it yet to be present with it in dignity and reality. The dreamer then received the naked sword as guardian to learn to wield it without using it. The paradox is *in losing, the dreamer won, yet in winning he lost*. Winning and losing become part of a total process with a single centre in which there is no winning or losing but only the balancing of energies.

In terms of dreamwork there is no absolute evil, adversity, destructiveness. *What makes something evil is resisting it.* The key principle in relating to adversarial forces is *to balance the energy*.

The above principles are revolutionary. All the time in dreams we resist adversaries. We fight them, run from them. The faster we run the more power we give to that which chases us. The harder we fight the more terrible the battle becomes. The more we destroy the more we are destroyed. There is something about resisting life which exaggerates life. *Resisting energy causes imbalance*. When you try to destroy your adversary you are trying to create an imbalance in the situation. When, instead of absolutely resisting, you maintain presence and balance the

86

power with your own, then a blending and a balancing can occur, the prelude to new unity and possible resolution.

Energy is always entering our sphere of existence. Sometimes we accept the energy and call it *good*. Other times we resist the energy by calling it *bad*. We are afraid the energy will hurt or destroy us, little realising that *whatever comes our way is life and can be dealt with*. The ego makes value judgments. It identifies with certain energies and rejects other energies. It has not learned to encompass the whole. This is the basis for all ethical systems which judge things good and bad. What the ego likes it calls good. What threatens it the ego calls bad. You do not need theologians, philosophers, and prophets to elaborate on this fundamental dynamic. What exists is real, is neither good nor bad, but is yet to be dealt with.

57. WE HEAL ADVERSARIAL DREAMS BY GOING THROUGH THE ISSUES TO COMPLETION.

Example: A woman who had been recently diagnosed as having breast cancer and was having to choose to go through major surgery dreamed she was at a social gathering. She picked up an hors d'oeuvre and was about to eat it when she saw it was a tiny, wriggling snake on a cracker. This so freaked her out that in anger and fear she threw the hors d'oeuvre across the room. (Amplifying dream heightening her actual life condition.)

Comment: Of course her condition is life-threatening, yet what we have is the inability yet to accept the full adversity in the situation. The dreamer would like to destroy her fate, the snake, as it is. The dreamer expresses her feelings. She does not want to lose her breasts, her youth, her beauty, her life. Yet is this reality? *Reality is our best teacher. Reality is what grounds us in the real. Reality is the great adversary to the ego.* The dream source seems to want her to face her condition so she no longer resists the process yet accepts it and makes the best choices possible. This she went on to do, studying her case thoroughly, and making the choice to go through with the surgery. She also changed her lifestyle by finally doing what she was meant to do vocationally and in terms of relationships.

58. WE USE DREAMWORK TO HEAL THE DREAM ITSELF.

Healing the dream means helping or allowing a dream to go to a natural resolution. *Healing occurs by bringing resolution to conflicts caused by trauma, physical and mental.* Either the organ returns to

THE ELEMENTS OF DREAMWORK

its natural function or it dies, sometimes taking the body with it. The psychological functioning either becomes expressive and integrative or dies, sometimes taking the person's vital personality with it.

Dreamwork can have powerful healing effects. The technique of Dream Re-entry has been successfully used by the author and his students in dealing with trauma blocks associated with recurrent nightmares. These traumas include rape, accident, war. Dream Re-entry, when done skilfully as a process, is in the author's experience one of the most powerful healing techniques developed in the twentieth century. Jung discovered that Ignatius Loyola, the founder of the Jesuits, used a form of guided imagery for religious renewal in the sixteenth century. Jung's own contribution, calling it *active imagination*, was to ask patients to use *Carrying the Dream Forward*, the author's term for a meditative technique in which the dreamer closes her eyes and allows images to develop out of the ending of the remembered dream, yet he was apparently against changing the dream itself by going back into it. The present author discovered dreamers could re-enter their dreams at the beginning and re-experience them to resolution without moving out of the original dream scenes, and this would produce healing effects in the dream situation and in the dreamer. (See Chapter 6, Dream Re-entry).

Healing war trauma through dreamwork

Example: A veteran had the following recurring dream for ten years after his war experience. He dreamed he was in Vietnam and heard the afternoon helicopters flying into the base with the day's casualties. He went to the chapel and got his ritual objects to give last rites to the dead Catholic soldiers, then he would go on to the hospital and was about to go through a door when he would wake. (Recurrent nightmare or Trauma dream in that it presents recurrent imagery which ends abruptly in a block.)

Comment: The dreamer could never get through the door in his recurrent dream. One time years later while walking he heard a helicopter overhead, went into a trance, and had the dream. He had developed diabetes and was up and down all night, every night. He thought he had become diabetic so he would have to wake throughout the night to prevent himself from having this horrible nightmare. The author did the following Guided Dream Re-entry with him which led to a cure of his nightmares and the return to a full sleep pattern.

The Dream Re-entry: The war veteran was asked to close his eyes and go into a meditative state and there see and experience his dream. This he did, again going for his last rites ritual objects from the chapel when the helicopters started coming in with the afternoon's wounded and dying. He came to the door and hesitated. This time he was asked if he could try to go through the door and describe whatever he saw there on the other side. He completed this quickly and reported that in the room were a number of soldiers on stretchers being bandaged by the nurses and doctors. Then he left. It was suggested he might return and focus on whatever seemed important to him in the room. He found a man with his head bandaged lying on a table. Seeing the medallion he wore indicating he was Catholic, he tried to move the bandage a little to see if he would recognise him and was told by the doctor to leave the bandage alone or the man's brains would fall out. Yet the priest recognised the soldier as one he had talked with two weeks earlier. They had told each other how they each were going home soon and the man showed the priest a picture of his wife and small daughter. The man was not going home alive. He died in front of the priest who gave him last rites for the dead. This was the trauma which had locked in the priest's unconscious, making him afraid to dream. To finish the Dream Re-entry, it was suggested he go to the chapel and have a dialogue with his God and even be angry there. Finally he could ask, Why? Why God does this happen in the world you created?

Comment: After coming out of this moving Dream Re-entry we had a conversation in which I suggested that somehow he had to include the presence of evil in the scheme of creation. Not to do so had led to his blocking out the horror of what he had experienced. His psyche wanted healing so badly it gave him nightmares. Facing his trauma with help led to healing. *He could not explain God yet he could accept reality.* Not to do so would keep the wound festering forever. *There are no answers to why questions, only responses that deal with things as they are.*

59. DREAMWORK HELPS US UNDERSTAND THE SYMBOLIC NATURE OF OUTER SITUATIONS

Many of us often feel we know what is happening out there in the 'real world'. We think we recognise who we are relating to, why we eat a certain food, what we are doing in our work situation, why we watch a certain programme on television. We are identified with what we do. *Identification* is when you experience yourself as the activity you do. For example, you are watching a sunset, yet are you watching the sun go down or experiencing the ending of life, not only the end of your day but someday your own final demise? Watching a beautiful sunset can evoke a sense of transcendence, of ending knowing also there will be a rebirth in the next dawn. Experiencing things symbolically as well as literally lets us be aware of the inner as well as the outer. The dream journey can mean *taking back what is out there and integrating it as within ourselves*. Learning dreamwork we learn to see the whole world as a dream and not simply a literal manifestation. Experiencing the *symbolic*, or inner significance of things, gives us a tremendous measure of freedom in choosing how we will relate to an event or person. When you are in love are you in love with that other person or a projected part of yourself? When you are in hate are you hating the other person or a projected part of yourself? The truth is in your dreams, the arena of the symbolic behind the actual.

Example: A nurse who worked in a hospital dreamed she was faced with many dead and dying people. She picked over the lot to recover the one person who might get well. In the next part of her dream she was making love with a beautiful woman and experiencing the warmth and intimacy of it. (Both a Compensatory and Revelatory dream compensating the outer situation and pointing to a creative attitude and solution in dealing with the conflict.)

Comment: To what does this dream refer? Using our method of contrasts and parallels, (see Chapter 6, Objectifying Dreams) we would see what the motifs or themes are in the dream and observe whether they parallel outer life situations. The week previous to this dream the dreamer had been giving morphine for pain relief to someone at the death stage of cancer. She informed the doctor that the amount of medication was depressing the blood pressure of the patient. She was acutely aware her actions could push this and other patients over the edge. The doctor told her the medication was right and the patient died.

Issue: Is this murder, and by whom, the doctor or the nurse, who both knew they were helping end a person's life? Or is this enlightened choice in which those with power aid a dying process and therefore are enhancing a person's life process, not to live but to die? *Dying is as much a part of living as is birthing*. At the end we are only alive to live our dying.

Comment: The dream shows the dreamer's attitude as being on the side of life, of saving those patients who are salvageable and letting the rest go. It also shows a major ethical dilemma for today's medical profession. They have an unrealistic and biased attitude in favour of life at all costs and so try to reverse the dying process in many patients, thereby causing additional suffering and *doing great disrespect to someone who is dying.* This dreamer must deal with this issue daily. Through dreamwork she is realising what her unconscious medical bias has been and her need now to include acceptance of *dying as being as natural a process as living.* She is changing her attitude towards keeping patients alive and helping them and their loved ones go through a dying process with consciousness and acceptance. Thus the dream shows what is symbolically going on behind the specific medical practices in a hospital, and offering choice and meaning to the dreamer. Would the whole medical profession could be trained in working with their dreams so as to better relate to the inner significance of their important outer work! Why must we continue to spend enormous sums on the latest diagnostic equipment and not some decent money on creating a dreamwork process room fully staffed to be used by anyone who steps through the door of a hospital?

It would be quite easy to have a confidential weekly staff dream group for sharing dreams and issues regarding work. Only when society takes a strong interest in the inner workings of its members will it be able to call itself civilised. *Consciousness, not technology, is the mark of a mature culture.*

And what about the dreamer making love to another woman in her dream? She felt the experience as healing, as warm, and full of life. Normally she mates with males in outer life, yet here she is experiencing sexuality as a re-contact with the feminine fertility spirit of life, a healthy counterbalance to dealing so much with death in her vocation. She sometimes feels strong sexual desire for certain friends or relatives of a dying person. This is natural and needs to be seen as symbolic, as the life force showing itself in counterbalance to the death force in her work.

As a general rule *dreams use the symbolism of our vocations to present to us the inner dynamics and attitudes evoked within ourselves by the outer situation.* Use Objectifying Dreams (see Chapter 6) to find out what is being evoked. How does what is happening in the dream parallel or contrast with what is happening in a similar situation in outer life?

60. BEING UNABLE TO SLEEP IS OFTEN DUE TO A NEED TO PROCESS REPRESSED MATERIAL REQUIRING EXPRESSION.

As we have seen, repressed material will come up in dreams, yet it will also let its presence be known by the inability to sleep at night. The cure is not sleeping pills but working through to resolution the feelings and dynamics evoked by life.

Solutions: Keep a dream and waking journal. If you are afraid or are having trouble sleeping, write about your feelings and issues. Get the material out of your head and on to paper so you can fall gently into sleep. Write your dreams down and work with them, even in the middle of the night. Create while the energy is there.

What you should not do: Take sleeping pills or tranquillisers, unless of course you need to be under the direct care of a healer or physician. Do not try to get back to sleep by lying there, reading, watching TV, masturbating, and other attempts at relaxation. If you are experiencing mild insomnia, then certain of the above methods may help release energy for you. Yet for major sleeplessness the only conscious way is to confront your issues and process them through. Work in your journal now, not later – yes, in the middle of the night.

61. HEALING ONESELF MEANS RESOLVING INNER BLOCKS AND EVOKING INTEGRATION IN ONESELF AND IN ONE'S LIFE.

Often people are in doubt as to what they should do with their lives or what they are like. They depend on others' evaluations of them to give a sense of self. They identify with outer roles to further define themselves to themselves. To be so extended outside oneself can lead to missteps in life, and to a one-sided personality. Dream people work with their dreams to find out who they are and how they operate. They are discovering and using inner knowledge.

When we relate to and heal the inner our relation to the outer will also improve. Inner is prior to outer. An inner house divided against itself cannot stand up to the outer vicissitudes of life.

Example: The dreamer dreamed she had to get in a lift going up a steep mountain. Once at the top she felt abandoned, for there seemed no way down and no one to help her. Then a woman appeared and proceeded to go down the mountain without any trouble. The dreamer went after her, the descent feeling natural and needing no particular effort. She was happy, for she had received help and had saved herself by following a guide. (Revelatory and Compensatory dream which shows the problem and the solution.)

Comment: The dreamer is in despair. She has gone into the unknown and is afraid she will not be able to cope with it. She does not trust yet there are always new resources for new problems. The fact that she received help in the dream carried into her waking life. She did recognise she could go into an unknown future relying, not on the known, but on the new resources which would come her way. In four months of intensive dreamwork at our institute this dreamer went through a dream transformation process. She left again for her home country in Europe with commitment and passion for new life, including working with dreams, her own and those of other people.

Every problem in life has its own solution, yet if we focus only on the problem we will never find the solution.

62. THE NEED FOR HEALING IS ULTIMATELY A SPIRITUAL ISSUE

Example: A woman early in her therapy dreamed she was rising to the surface in a small submarine. When she broke the surface she cried out, 'Oh God how glorious are your works. I will follow your will and honour the child.' (Spiritual Issues dream highlighting the ego's commitment to the work.)

Comment: A number of issues are raised by this dream. Certainly the feeling quality is different if someone remains immersed in the deeps. Here her prognosis is good. Even though her vessel is small she has one and reaches the surface where she is, in a burst of feeling, able to acknowledge Source energies, which some people call God. We use the generic more functional terms to distinguish the energy from a religious concept. The dreamer feels redeemed and offers praise and commitment. Praise without commitment lacks realism and integrity. When you reach the surface into some consciousness then the next phase of the work begins, which is a conscious commitment to practise what you have learned through suffering and necessity. Most people will work hard if they are suffering. The ones who also have a spiritual passion will work commitedly for the love of the life and meaning which can result. To follow the will of God spiritually rather than religiously, is to place one's ego within the service of a larger value than itself, a source far superior in wisdom and energy than the ego has. The ego keeps sacrificing its hold on itself to find Source, that which it is not but makes it more than it is. The child could represent also the new life. You do not follow a spiritual direction just to follow it, but to realise new life, the Child Archetype, a central symbol of wholeness and new meaning.

SUMMARY

We have come to the end of our exploration of the dark side as it is dealt with in dreams, dreamwork, and in life. We as people are naturally on the side of life, health, and wealth, based most certainly on our survival instinct built up through our evolutionary struggle. Yet to survive in a complex world we must learn how to include adversity within the wholeness process rather than resist it. *Resisting something makes it destructive.* Including it within a circle of possible transformation allows the destroying force, the archetype of adversity, to have its natural place. For two of the great archetypes of existence are the opposites, Adversity and Heroic, destroying and saving, bad and good, negative and positive. These come together at the locus of the Self, the integrative centre, within struggle and conflict. Conflict in life is natural and we must deal with it if we are to be both effective and whole. Dreams are continually presenting us in conflicting situations, as if saying, deal with it, give up control and resistance and balance the energy confronting you. We have also seen how the powerful dreamwork techniques of Dream Re-entry and Dream Enactment help dreamworkers face their great emotional blocks and deal with them, often creating healing resolutions. We need a change of attitude and a commitment to accept the dark side as part of reality and to keep processing what comes up. This suggests the basic principle and practise that *there is a creative solution to every problem if we would but face the problem and deal with it fully.* Greater then than the achieving of happiness is the achieving of wholeness, the integration of opposites and the fulfilment and meaning that creates.

THINGS TO DO

- What is healing to you? List some of the conflicts in your dreams and in life and see how the two lists form parallels. Then for each set devise choices you might make to resolve these situations in life and in dreams. You can even do Rewriting the Dream to resolve certain dream situations as practise for taking steps to resolve outer situations as well.

- What is your commitment to remembering and recording your dreams? Do you tend to remember only the important ones? Try and record any dream without first evaluating it, or reacting against it. Then have your feelings. Read again the dream at the end of the day.

- What are your attitudes and practises regarding difficulties in life and dreams? Describe them. Review the principles in this chapter and see which you can adopt to practise in dreams and life. Write about them, even keeping track in your journal of what develops.

- Research your dreams to find some intense ones in which you are trying to keep the adversary out or avoid him or her. What does this say about yourself? Now consider how you might stay present more to the dream adversaries, and even let them in and interact with you. Yes, feel the feelings, and seek support if you are afraid of being overwhelmed.

- Work out your basic attitude or principle which can include the opposites of adversity and healing, the negative and positive together. Then work out a practice for living out your principle in dreams and in life.

- What is your commitment to wholeness, to including and integrating everything within the framework of a meaningful life? What do your dreams and dreamwork challenge you to in terms of your own wholeness process?

- What are your dreams telling you about your own violence and evil? Look for the crimes and hidden things, the shame, the bizarre, the violent, the stealing, the sexual extravaganzas. What is your dream ego's relation to all this? Now how do the dynamics and issues you are discovering relate to your outer life? What will it take to include the dark side in your life? What kind of commitment to wholeness can you make?

- Pick out certain of your dreams which need healing and do dreamwork with them. You can see what the issues are, and changes in behaviour you as dream ego can make. Then do Rewriting the Dream or Dream Re-entry or even Dream Enactment with a dream to help evoke a healing resolution. Use support in this work. Adversity is real.

- Look in your dreams to see what adversity and potential for healing is there in terms of outer situations of work and relationship. Note the parallels and contrasts. Create life tasks for acting more effectively and meaningfully in the outer.

- Review your sleep habits and patterns. Do you want to write in your journal every night and other times when you have issues and energy to process? Make commitments to tasks more important than sleep.

- Who are the helpers in your dreams and how do they help you? What is your dream ego relation to them? Resistance? Thankfulness? Acceptance? Other? How do you use help in your life? What help is needed now, especially in dealing with the difficult? What is the process you regularly use to deal with difficult things in yourself, in others, in life?

- What are the issues evoked for you by this chapter on Healing and Adversity? Write to them. Read the chapter again. Let it challenge you. See what the dreams bring, as well as what your fate sends you. Accept! Integrate!

6 · THE MAJOR DREAMWORK METHODS

These methods serve to actualise dreams, not interpret them. If you have a methodology you do not need a dogma. For with method you create and focus experience. You live in the real world of action and being, not in an ideal world of intellect and fantasy. We do use our intellects and imagination in experiencing the light and the dark, but we bring this energy into concrete reality wherein we find our grounding. The methods are practical to use, and they evoke the source from which dreams seem to come. *We cannot learn from experience unless we are committed to doing the work.*

INDIVIDUAL DREAMWORK

Individual dreamwork can often be done effectively on one's own by studying this approach and using the methods on one's dreams. Basic is keeping a dream journal and committing yourself to recording dreams and working with them at least once a week. In a year you will have the wealth of over fifty dreamwork projects completed. To help support the process, you might ask a friend to meet regularly, even over lunch, to share the dreamwork you have each done. Better to share dreamwork than to share only dreams, for then you make yourself do the work in preparation for the meeting. Make it regular and you will go further with the process. After some experience, read the book again, making notes where inspired. It will be a different read this time. Good luck! Then at some point you may want to travel to a dreamwork intensive.

DREAM GROUP DREAMWORK

The dream group experience is a group which meets weekly or bi-weekly with or without an experienced leader for around two hours. If all members of a group agree to work from this book they will be equipped to do basic work on dreams. Each member of from three to eight people is encouraged to share a dream with time to work with some of the dreams. Other formats for a dream group are meeting on a residential weekend once a month or every other month. The present form the author's dreamwork training takes is a year's commitment to intensive training involving five four-day residential trainings every two months plus a ten-day summer dreamwork intensive. (See also the author's *The Dreamwork Manual*.)

Step by step method

1. Organise and try to get at least three months' commitment to the work. Set regular times. Each person start or continue a dream journal and record as many dreams as possible. Bring the dream journal to each session.

2. Start meditatively in a circle in chairs or on pillows in a place where you will not be interrupted. Some groups light the dream candle in the centre. No eating or drinking during dream group. Socialise before or after so that the focus is on serious work.

3. Take turns sharing a dream and give comments. Then other members of the group can ask questions of the dreamer to *objectify* the dream and make clear how the *dream ego* is acting or not acting in the dream. Do not focus mainly on the person's outside life. *Stay with the dream and what is happening in the dream.* Help a perspective develop. Work meditatively so that there is time to feel. *Do not interpret* another's dream either as dream group leader or participant. This projects your issues into someone else's dream. *Turn 'insight' into possibility by asking a question.* Also suggest dream tasks which the person might do there or later. Relate the dream to previous work. The dreamer can also share how they worked with their dream. Somebody can volunteer to watch the time for each person and signal when it is time to move on.

4. *Dreamwork* can be done with some of the shared dreams, and this takes longer. Use this book and you will have a grounded experience. Also, the whole group can spend the first part of at least some sessions working on a *technique for the week*. Pick the method and use it right there, then share results. This will train members so if they choose to keep meeting they will have a more ready skill in the techniques.

5. If a leader does the group, follow the same procedure, but usually be the first one to ask questions of the dreamer to help bring out key issues. Then call for response from others. *Do dreamwork rather than interpretation. Let wisdom come from the work, not the leader.* Keep track of the time and the dream. Write up the experience afterwards. On the left you as leader put what was evoked for you personally by the process. On the right you include other people's experience and their dreams. This is good processing and another way of learning dreamwork. Charge for your work. This acknowledges your value to the group and the value of the dreamwork to the participants. *What you charge is in part a measure of your self esteem and how much you value dreamwork.*

Effects

• Dream group experience provides an acceptance of dreams and support in going through the dreamwork process. Through relating to each others' dreams and dreamwork members experience the richness of the unconscious, the spiritual journey, the courage and feeling in the work together and separately.

• Each dream shared and worked with becomes in part everyone's dream. We each gain something important from someone else's dream and therefore are ourselves more whole.

• We form a relatedness with others which is real and has a spiritual base, the working with source energies which do not originate from ego. There are many ways to relate in life. *What we choose is what we become.*

• We gain direct support for doing dreamwork in the group and on our own. *It strengthens commitment to have somewhere to go.* The structure enables us. Even if we resist going on a particular night, once there we will gain something meaningful.

KEEPING A DREAM JOURNAL

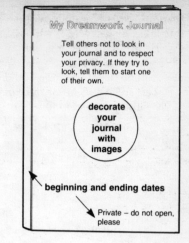

My Dreamwork Journal

Tell others not to look in
your journal and to respect
your privacy. If they try to
look, tell them to start one
of their own.

**decorate
your
journal
with
images**

beginning and ending dates

Private – do not open,
please

Figure 7

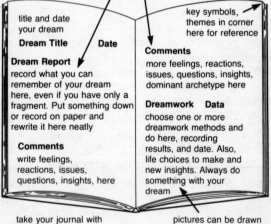

you can also write up high energy experiences in your dream journal
and process them like you would a dream, or in place of a dream

title and date
your dream

Dream Title   **Date**

Dream Report
record what you can
remember of your dream
here, even if you have only a
fragment. Put something down
or record on paper and
rewrite it here neatly

Comments
write feelings,
reactions, issues,
questions, insights, here

key symbols,
themes in corner
here for reference

Comments
more feelings, reactions,
issues, questions, insights,
dominant archetype here

Dreamwork   Data
choose one or more
dreamwork methods and
do here, recording
results, and date. Also,
life choices to make and
new insights. Always do
something with your
dream

take your journal with
you to work and cafes

pictures can be drawn
or pasted in as well

Figure 8   Writing in your dreamwork journal

REMEMBERING DREAMS

We remember dreams by actualising them. Your basic commitment is
to making concrete in some way what comes up from dreaming. If you

seem to remember nothing, then write down anything in your dream journal as you wake each morning. Anyone can write their thoughts upon waking while still in bed. Make sure you allow time for this before moving into the day's obligations.

Among the best methods for remembering dreams is to do the preparation for Dream Incubation the previous night. If you want a dream on a subject, then just before bed write your thoughts about that issue or subject, and end with a written request, either in your journal or on a piece of paper you place under your pillow. Also include that you would like to remember a dream in the morning and you will commit to writing down anything, dream or not, which is there in your awareness when you awake.

Be aware that many people have attitudes around remembering and writing down dreams. This is not school and an assignment which must be done well. Just write what comes and do the work you can. *Commitment is to the possible, not the impossible.*

Recalling important things has much to do with consciousness. Watch your negative motivation. Do you remember things you have to do because you are anxious about them? Recalling dreams needs to come from positive motivation. You look forward to seeing what you dreamed in the night because your dreams are important and full of messages from some deep part of you. Besides, some dreams are fun, exciting, scary, mysterious. Why wouldn't we want to remember such a creative part of ourselves?

If you are blocking on remembering your dreams you may be resisting, afraid that things will come up which seem dark and overwhelming. Yes, the dark side does come up in dreams because *dreams are more whole, more honest, than we are.* Committing to remembering and writing down dreams is an initial commitment to experiencing and working with whatever the Dream Source chooses to reveal to you. Yes, your commitment will also need to be towards removing and transforming the blocks in you which prevent the fullness of life and destiny.

Try waking yourself every morning without the use of the alarm. Use it only for backup. This way you are training yourself to wake consciously, remembering to awake, and to remember a dream. Dreams generally come every one-and-a-half hours, so either wake after six hours' sleep or seven-and-a-half, not the traditional eight hours' sleep!

Put interesting books and things under your pillow to dream about. It works!

If all else fails, wake yourself each one-and-a-half hours with the alarm, write down anything which is there, and pour a glass of water. Have the pitcher and four glasses handy. Do not ask why, just do it and see what results.

We only need to remember what we tend to forget. The rest is simply natural recall.

OBJECTIFYING DREAMS

Objectifying Dreams sees the dream in its dream report as a natural thing in itself to be explored like any poem, play, or piece of art. Most approaches and people do not stay long with the dream. They either leap off from the dream into life, or impose some symbol system on to it in an attempt to control the dream experience. Instead, we stay with the dream, look at it closely, see what its internal structures are, what the dream ego is and is not doing, what the chief symbols and actions are, and how they are related or not related to each other in the dream. We use the Laws of Similarity and Contrast to help recognise these structures. We do not interpret by referring to outside things such as mythology, past lives, dream dictionaries, opinions, what happened the previous day, what is occurring in your life right now. Since the dream is already full of images and actions in unusual embrace it is easy to project on to dreams or try to control them with rational statements, turning symbol into concept. We use objectifying each time we work in depth with a dream. As you practise the process will go much faster. Objectifying is also excellent when applied to life situations as well.

Step by step method

1. Use the Laws of Similarity and Contrast. List all the things which are similar in the dream. Then list all the contrasts you can come up with. You are not trying to explain why the dream happened this way, just seeing what the actual dream is like.

2. Now list the relationships between symbols, between symbols and actions, between the dream ego and the symbols and actions in the dream. *A dream action is also a symbol just as an image is.* One is static, one is moving, one is being, one is doing, one is potential, one is action.

3. List what the dream ego is doing and not doing in the dream. How strong are its relationships with other things in the dream, and what is the nature of the relationships?

4. Describe the progression from beginning to end. Is there a *setting* of the scene, a *development* of the action, a constellation of the *issues*, *a crisis*, or potential *blocking* point, around a *tension between opposites*, and finally a *resolution* or *need for resolution*? List each of these.

5. Finally make a summary statement of the main things you have discovered.

6. Objectifying Dreams sets the stage for further work. You can do Key Questions by listing all the questions and issues you can. Dialogueing with Dream Figures might come from recognising the greatest issue being presented in the dream and picking what turns out to be the major symbol to dialogue with. Dream Re-entry and Symbol Immersion would be based on knowing the key symbols and issues and re-entering the dream to activate and deal with them further. Rewriting the Dream would also do this.

7. The effects are principally new consciousness about the dream's issues and dynamics, and the clearing away of projections on to the dream. You are teaching yourself through dreamwork *to see things as they really are* instead of projecting on to them or resisting them through denial. This way you have to look carefully and be in the moment.

KEY QUESTIONS

Key Questions is an easy technique for bringing out the issues in a dream. Basically, you keep listing questions about your dream until you can mark key questions from the whole list and write to them, your dream affect you more. Do not stop to write responses to the questions unless the energy is so intense you have to. At the end you can mark key questions from the whole list and write them, either by direct spontaneous writing without thinking, or by doing dialogue with a dream figure and asking that being the questions and writing responses you hear in your inner ear. Use this method as preparation for Dialogueing with Dream Figures, after Objectifying Dreams, and as preparation for Dream Re-entry. The chief effect is to produce new consciousness.

Key questions to ask about things in your dreams

- What are the main issues of this dream?

- Why am I doing what I am doing in this dream?
- What do I most need to deal with in this dream?
- What are the similarities, what are the contrasts?
- What in this dream is related to things in other dreams I have had?
- What in this dream is related to what is going on in me or in my life right now?
- What is it about this dream I most resist?
- What most inspires me?
- What is being asked of me by this dream?
- What am I needing to look at, and even make a choice about, that I had to have this dream?
- How can I actualise this dream so that it can become more real?

FOLLOWING THE DREAM EGO

Following the Dream Ego is a method where you focus directly on what your dream ego, the image of you in the dream, is or is not doing. From this research you then probe deeper to the underlying feelings and attitudes. The regular practice of this technique will enable you to follow the progression of dream ego behaviour and attitude change over a series of dreams. You will gain direct feedback of improvement and change in your activity in the dream state and in outer life. Following the Dream Ego also lays the basis for making changes in outer life waking ego behaviour, and for having those changes confirmed in new dream ego behaviour in future dreams. You are developing your consciousness in one of the most effective ways there is by using your dream ego to reflect you back to yourself.

When to use

- Use every fourth dream to keep a continual check on yourself in dreams and life.
- When you commit to the task of finding out who you are as a distinct person rather than as a member of a group, relationship, or lifestyle.
- Use to lay the basis for becoming more active in your dreams while

dreaming them.

- This technique, along with Objectifying Dreams, creates the basis for in depth dreamwork vial Dialogueing with Dream Figures, Dream Re-entry, or Dream Enactments.

- When you need to do quick and clear dreamwork. If the whole rest of a dream is unclear to you, you will always receive immediate feedback by responding to the question, what is my dream ego doing or not doing in this dream, and why?

Step by step method

1. Objectify the dream, at least briefly, to get at the key structures and actions the dream seems to embody.

2. List all the dream ego's main actions in the dream as what it did do and what it did not do.

3. Then pick a key action and list what attitude might be motivating that action. An *attitude* is an unconscious context for choice. You may have to work at this one, for it seems almost an impossible task for the ego to reflect upon itself. *Only the blind can lead the blind.* Attitudes are often stated as rules, shoulds, absolutes. There may be three or four different attitudes, or ways of stating them, behind a single dream ego action. You do not have to know which is the right one. Simply list them all. Ask for help from someone else who may be more able to see you clearly.

4. Once having got to the attitudes of two or three key actions, go on to feeling. *Feeling* is an energic reaction positive or negative. Positive, we approach. Negative, we withdraw. Often the dream action and symbol will be described in the dream report but not how the dream ego felt in the moment about the action occurring. List what feelings the dream ego expressed, what feelings you felt it had but did not express, and what feelings you would give to the dream ego now. With every action there is always an appropriate feeling. Feeling is not perception but reaction. Feeling leads to action. Perception leads to stillness and distancing in the observer role. This is an incomplete list of typical feelings, *like, dislike, fear, enthusiasm, frustration, warmth, cold, despairing, sadness, insecure, momentarily angry, loving, lost, accepted, hurt, vital, shy, joyful, dreadful, terror, awe, moved by meaning, bored, hollow, wonderful, awful, creative, inspired.* Pick from this list and add feelings of your own.

5. List also the emotions the dream ego is expressing, is having but not expressing, or would be appropriate to have and express in the situation. An emotion is not generally a feeling, since its intensity and tone overrides the moment and any specific other feelings which might be there. Emotions are of long duration. *Emotion is repressed or undifferentiated feeling.* One task in dream and life work is to get the emotion released so that the person can have feelings. Some emotions are, *anger, love, hate, inflationary joy or depression, despondency or despair which lasts and lasts, bitchiness, complaining, criticalness, pushiness and bullying, anxiety, spaciness, resistance, paranoia, murderous, grief, bitterness.* Suffering is not used as a feeling or emotion but is a function which expresses feeling and emotion. The dream ego may or may not be expressing these emotions, so it is important to make a list here also of what it is and is not expressing.

6. Once having listed some of the feelings and emotions that have been expressed or not expressed by the dream ego, take one or two of the important ones and analyse to see whether these energy states are producing the attitudes which motivate the actions or non-actions, or whether the attitudes are producing the feelings and attitudes. We cannot always tell which comes first, but it helps to know to induce change.

7. Our immediate goal is to become a lot clearer on how our dream ego acts and interacts and why. Most people blame others and situations as the cause of their reactions to situations. The outside is not the determining cause but only an insistent factor. What determines our behaviour is the stuff below the surface of consciousness, the attitudes and patterns overriding our lives expressed through compulsive unconscious behaviour.

8. To continue the change process, list new attitudes the dream ego can live by and the new actions it might take in the dream situation based on these more creative and meaningful attitudes. *Principles are attitudes consciously realised.* When we discover an unconscious attitude we evaluate it. Is this attitude effective in reality? Is it realistic? Does it work? What results are produced from enacting it, and are those the results I want for myself? Is this attitude meaningful? Is it consistent with the life I choose to live? Often attitudes are unconscious because they were shovelled into us as children by parents and other authority figures, or they are the result of intense childhood experiences, usually traumatic. *To*

change the effects of childhood we must get to the attitudes as well as the unconscious patterns also created.

9. Change the inadequate attitudes by creating affirmations from them. To create an affirmation you rewrite the attitude keeping some of its reality but putting in some new value or concept which makes it more realistic or meaningful.

10. Adopt new principles for living the same dream or life situation. Principles can come from wisdom sources, and from our dreams. Take a dream scene you deem creative and rewrite the imagery as a principle or attitude. Dreams are wisdom in imagery. Creating principles is one good way to turn image into concept. Also summarise your dreamwork experiences by bringing them to essence in a one sentence statement written as a principle or short teaching. Live this in your life and dreams.

11. Now having done all this work, you are ready to Rewrite the Dream if you so choose. Take the new principle or attitude and as dream ego live it in the same dream situation but allowing the imagery and feeling to shift in response to the new behaviour. This could bring a sense of resolution to the dream issue or situation. The two other methods you can use here are Dream Re-entry or Dream Enactment.

12. Summarise your process in your dream journal and possibly share with another person who would have some understanding of dreamwork.

13. To do a short form of this process, take only one important dream interaction by the dream ego and go through this procedure step by step, but skipping places where you feel confused. Skip and continue. Start somewhere. *Doing a little can be better than doing nothing at all.*

Effects

- You become conscious of inner motivation and no longer blame outside factors for how you behave.

- You become conscious of how you act in dreams and life and what motivates you.

- You become much more effective and value-centred by consciously choosing what principles and attitudes you will live by.

- This method sometimes scares people because of the thinking work involved. Thinking used in the service of a deep process adds a conscious dimension not accomplished by feeling. We have included important feeling techniques in this book. Now for some thinking work to balance the process!

REWRITING THE DREAM

In Rewriting the Dream you take your original dream and search out its issues. You see how your dream ego could have better acted in the dream. In rewriting you write the dream with your dream ego more active and creative, letting the rest of the dream energy change as it will in response.

When to use

- When a dream issue or scene needs resolving, or when Dream Re-entry would seem too scary.

- When you need to practise resolving issues in your dreams and in life in a healthy way.

Step by step method

1. Determine key issues by using these techniques: Objectifying Dreams, Following the Dream Ego, and Key Questions.

2. Choose for yourself a stance or attitude that you would like your dream ego to embody.

3. Take pen in hand and write as rapidly as possible, keeping the new behaviour of the dream ego in mind and letting the rest of the dream's imagery develop as it will. Write until you feel a natural resolution to the dream.

4. Evaluate your experience by contrasting the original dream with the rewritten dream. What new attitudes, principles, and ways of acting have been born?

5. Apply what you have learned to a similar outer life situation if appropriate.

6. Perhaps share your results with another person to further affirm what you are doing.

DIALOGUES WITH DREAM FIGURES

Dialogue is inner conversation with the dream energies embodied in the dream figures. These may be parts of ourselves which are different from our waking egos. There may also be *spiritual entities*, or energy centres which exist but which do not strictly inhabit the individual psyche. Sometimes a dialogue does seem transpersonal in part as coming from a deep wisdom source or from the essence of someone who has died. If there is a psychic factor, then dialogue may help us use that function to find life wisdom. Who can argue with the results regardless of the theory to explain it?

When to use

- Use to make conscious the dream symbol by having these figures talk back to the ego part of yourself.

- Use to bring resolution to issues presented in dreams. A dialogue which gets a flow going takes off on its own with new information coming in which feels like a resolution to the issue.

- Use to increase the relatedness between parts of yourself symbolised by dream figures. This is conscious relating which is also a letting go process. It aids wholeness and healing to connect the ego function up with other dynamics in the psyche.

Step by step method

1. The first step is to do at least in part, Objectifying the Dream, Following the Dream Ego, and Key Questions. This will bring out the issues to dialogue around.

2. To clear the channels, at least for the first time, do first a dialogue with the Dialogue Censor. This dynamic represents the Judge, that part of us which says, this is nonsense. Acknowledge this part by coming to terms with it. Ask it who it is, what it wants, and what it will take to get it out of the way so that your dream dialogue can flow freely. This will produce good results, and you know whom to turn to if things again feel blocked.

3. Formulate two or three key questions to ask your dream figure. Write these down. Then begin the dialogue. Write quickly without thinking or evaluating. If you have reactions just let them be at the side and continue the expressing. Ask a key question and write whatever comes into your head. Then either give a feeling reaction back, or ask another question. Soon you should feel the flow and be asking questions spontaneously and giving reactions. Write until the dialogue feels complete or until the energy has run out or you feel blocked or enough has come up to deal with.

109

4. Read over what has been written. What was the issue and what was the response? How did you do as dialogue person? What about the Dialogue Censor? What was the resolution? What new perspective can be gained here? What are your doubts? What if you followed what has been said to you? How would your life be different? Do you value and choose this? Write it up in your dream journal.

Effects

- New consciousness about yourself and your dream is produced.

- A sense of resolution around some issue, dream induced, may have come about giving a sense of renewal from the work, or even breakthrough.

- Your own relations to inner sources has been further opened so that you can live more from inner wisdom tailored to you as a person.

- You will be helped to express more by letting go to creative sources.

- You may be shocked by dark material like swear words coming out. Do not censor, and you do not have to share this with anyone. This is the repressed shadow taking advantage of your willingness to let go and not be guarded. Let it have its say so you can also include it and move on.

DREAM TASKS

Dream Tasks are specific projects you commit to based on your dreams. Sometimes, even, the dream will have you as dream ego doing something new and creative, as if it itself wants you to try the new action. When through with a piece of dreamwork, bring its value to essence and further ground yourself by constructing specific changes in behaviour which you will make to live the new values and insights received through the dreamwork. Tasks can be simple projects like practising saying No if you habitually say Yes a lot. The effect of doing tasks is to make changes concrete and real. They are also tests to see how committed a person you are. Do you tell a good story, even have intensely emotional experiences, but are you also integrating and working to change the outer life as well? This whole book has been quite a Dream Task for me!

SYMBOL IMMERSION

In Symbol Immersion we take a key symbol or action from a dream, go into the meditative state with eyes closed, and meditate on the symbol. To do this you focus in on whatever you can see, however vague it might look, and describe it in the greatest detail possible, either to yourself or another. Stay focused on the symbol as it was in the dream, or as you see it now, and do not let it change. You want to hold the tension of staying with the symbol to experience it as fully as possible as it is. This gives you a non-thinking experience in itself, a direct path back to the Dream Source. When the tension has been held long enough you can let it change, if it will. Do not make it change. This is not rational, ego-controlled visualisation. The effect is to make your dream symbol more alive and to affect your unconscious patterns directly. This is a good technique for having dream fragments come alive, especially when doing a Guided Symbol Immersion.

DREAMBODY WORK

In Dreambody Work we focus on a scene or image from a dream while in a meditative state lying prone. After the imagery is vivid we want to bring it directly into bodily awareness as internal energy. Being hit in a dream can re-channel in Dreambody Work as energy pounding in the diaphragm. *The body is itself a dream, a symbolic entity with all its organs and places being centres of* energy. Most bodies which have not learned to release on a daily basis are armoured, tight, blocked, experiencing symptoms such as headaches. Along with these symptoms will be memory traces and patterns. So by going into bodily awareness via dream content we can see where the dream dynamic is also affecting our bodies. By focusing there we bring choice and awareness helping the block become open so that life energy can move freely in us. *Pleasure is when the life force flows freely. Pain is when the life force is blocked.* Dreambody Work can often lead to awareness and emotional release as tears, anger, trembling, or vomiting. Have plenty of tissues ready. The releasing of tension and old stuff is vital to the healing process. Dreams present the issues. They seldom heal us directly. That is what we must do in following and actualising the dream. (See also Arnold Mindel's *Process Psychology* and *Dreambody* books.)

ARCHETYPAL DREAMWORK

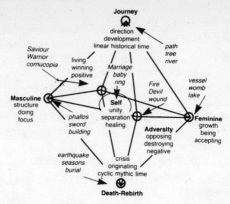

Figure 9 The Seven Basic Archetypes with key chief functions and images. Other images and functions of similar nature can be added to each of the archetypes.

Archetypal Dreamwork looks at which basic archetype seems dominant in a particular dream or a series of dreams. Often most of a person's dreams during a given period will have certain archetypes dominant and other archetypes absent. To counteract this imbalance the dreamer needs to evoke the opposite archetypal energy, thus evoking resolution and wholeness. Dreamers with too much Adversity will lack the Heroic in their dreams, for example.

Step by step method

1. Use the Seven Basic Archetypes model to place images and actions from your dream. You can even make a large drawing of the model and write in specific dream symbols and themes, showing over time which archetypes are most active in your psyche and life.

2. Determine also which archetypal dynamics your dream ego does and does not embody. What might be the creative result if it also expressed opposite archetypal characteristics different from its usual stance?

3. To affirm more wholeness in your dreams and life, which archetypal energy needs to be in your dreams and life to counterbalance the dominant dynamics in your recent dreams? Do Rewriting the Dream, Dream Enactment, or Dream Re-entry in ways which

can evoke the opposite energy as well as amplify the dominant archetypes. Focus also on the centralising functions of the Self, so that integration and healing may occur. Do not leave the Adversarial Archetype out!

Effects

- The effects of developing a wholeness process in your life can be vitalising. Most illness and issues are due to one-sidedness, in part created by the ego's identifying with one opposite to the detriment of the other.
- Working with this method will create an overview of how your own individuation and wholeness process is or is not working. It also trains you in the skills of counterbalancing energies in life so that you may better resolve issues.

DREAM RE-ENTRY

Dream Re-entry is one of the most powerful of healing dreamwork methods. It has its antecedents in the method of active imagination devised by C.G. Jung. But the technique as now practised has been modified and developed further at the Jungian-Senoi Institute under the direction of the author beginning in 1978.

Dream Re-entry is done by closing your eyes and going into a meditative state. The practitioner is asked to again see and describe the original dream scene and then to let the action proceed. Preparation for Dream Re-entry is accomplished by doing Objectifying Dreams, Following the Dream Ego, and Key Questions. These techniques help the dreamer become aware of how the dream ego is acting or not acting in the dream and what the key issues are, as embedded in the dream's dynamics. Focus especially on how you as dream ego might act more creatively in the Dream Re-entry. During re-entry the dream ego is more active, and imagery and other dynamics may change in ways which have not been created by the dreamer's ego. Dream Re-entry continues until the dream situation or conflict feels resolved or the process has come to a stopping place in which the dreamer cannot or does not wish to go on.

When to use

- When a dream issue or scene needs resolving.
- When you want to simply experience your dream more fully.
- When you want to evoke and process traumatic material reflected in the dream.
- When you want to explore a dream scene further than in the original experience.
- In order to train yourself through practise to become creatively active in dreams and life.

Step by step method

1. Determine key issues by using the techniques: Objectifying Dreams, Following the Dream Ego, and Key Questions.
2. Place yourself in a meditative state with your eyes closed and see in the present the chief dream scene you want to deal with. Describe to yourself or another all the details you see. Do not let the action develop yet.
3. Let the dream action proceed slowly. At the same time have your dream ego interact more creatively than in the original dream without seeking to change any of the dream's imagery or stop it from changing.
4. Allow and respond to the dream's imagery changing as your dream ego interacts with it.
5. Keep interacting with the dream imagery until a natural resolution to the dream situation seems to have developed. Then end the Dream Re-entry and come wide awake again.
6. Contrast and evaluate how this dream experience is different from your original dream experience.
7. Emphasise especially what has felt resolved in the Dream Re-entry and within the dreamer.
8. Write up your experience in your dream journal.

Guided Dream Re-entry (being guided often allows the dreamer to let go more and to participate in new ways.)

1. Follow the same procedure as for Self Dream Re-entry.
2. Let a skilled dreamwork practitioner guide you. The guide asks you every half minute or so, what is happening? This keeps the

dreamer alert. For the leader, do not ask how do you feel while the process is going on, as this makes the dreamer too aware of the waking ego.

3. The guide may suggest alternatives to choose at key transition points in the Dream Re-entry, but do not give the dreamer only one alternative. *The guide should not impose a direction on the experience.* This means, do not usually suggest specific things to do, new imagery, or to go in a certain direction. *Trust the Dream Source as to the direction for the process.*

4. The dream ego can interact directly with dream figures and situations, and sometimes also enter into a dialogue with them or the situation. Keep asking questions and you will get a fuller response.

5. Go through the procedure to the end as you continually report to your guide what you are experiencing in the dream and in your body.

6. When resolution occurs come out of the dream state slowly and open your eyes and look around. Work in your journal about your experience if the energy feels right for it. The guide can also process his or her own experience.

7. Apply the changes in being and attitude to a life situation where you can test out what you have learned.

Effects

- Often the dreamer will feel differently after a re-entry. This means that a pattern below consciousness has been unblocked so that new life and imagery can flow.

- New dream imagery will usually manifest itself spontaneously.

- Sometimes the dreamer may feel dizzy or ungrounded. While still in the meditative state focus awareness in one's body. Lower the intensity of energy down from the head into the guts and sometimes lower into the ground.

- Deep feelings may be evoked. Make sure resolution of the dream's conflict is occurring so that the person will not end up feeling blocked.

- Sometimes the person may come to a dangerous or blocked place in the dream. Suggest interventions when seriously needed, such as introducing a healing symbol or strong figure the person

115

knows. Create tools and allies for dealing with the potentially overwhelming situation.

- A sense of healing and meaning can happen after such a process. Encourage a sensitive sharing but do not interrupt the experience or its mood. Do not articulate into words the deep feelings aroused unless the person needs or wants a perspective. We want the effect to remain as it is, and not put it into concepts but kept as a feeling.

- You may dream another dream confirming your new dream behaviour. When this happens it is as if the Dream Source likes your new way of dealing with the issue and confirms it, often with an added touch or challenge.

- You will grow in your ability to bring resolution to various issues in life by practising resolving issues in your dreamwork.

DREAM ENACTMENT

Dream Enactment is taking some aspect of the dream and acting it out either alone or in the group. Dream Enactment helps us actualise the actions and potentials of the dream in such a way that we feel them, thus effecting healing by changing underlying patterns which insight alone would not change. Sometimes this is called Dream Theatre or Dream Drama, but these last two names are reserved for a more formal presentation of a dream. In Dream Enactment we take the key dream action and act it out symbolically, being careful at the end to also bring resolution and consciousness to the experience.

Caution: This is not for the inexperienced. Strong leadership should be provided by a well-trained therapist and dreamworker who does process well. *Do not evoke what you are unwilling to contain and transform.*

When to use

Use this technique to help the healing process occur at a deep emotional level beyond the conscious control. It gets one into feelings and archetypal patterns where true process can happen. Use also to utilise the group's support in carrying out the work. They love the involvement. *A dream enacted is never forgotten.*

Step by step method

1. First interact with the person after they tell the dream, objectifying the dream and getting to the key issues with them. Ask what they

most want to work on, and then pick a scene, a main part of the dream.

2. Most enactments should last five to fifteen minutes so that there are breakthroughs, but without becoming lost in the drama of the dream or the person's life. The leader designs a simple key dream scene with the dreamer and asks the dreamer to choose the people to fill the three or four roles. The dreamer usually plays the dream ego. The dream group leader directs but does not usually enact.

3. First bring those involved out of the room so they can become clear on their parts and get into their feelings. The rest of the group is the audience. You have prepared an area as the staging place. Then the director goes back in first and the others come when ready. Do not spend too long preparing. *This is not a performance but an imperfect reality.*

4. Enact the dream scene as it was in the original dream. The process here is to amplify the key symbolic dynamics. Do not let the people do voice dialogues, as this makes things too conscious. We want primary interactions and movements. The director helps the whole experience move physically and emotionally until at some point it takes off.

5. During the enactment the leader enhances key movements which seem central, thus amplifying major elements without making a specific thing happen. If the process seems slow or becomes blocked have the other enactors do a few more things. You may ask the dreamer, what is going on?, and encourage the person to let go. When the scene is over, stop the action and ask questions of the dreamer like, what happened for you? What feels still unresolved? What would you like to do differently?

6. This time you do the enactment again but with a healing resolution. Often dreams present only issues and not resolutions. *To evoke resolution is the conscious task of the awake ego.* You have become clear with the dreamer what the real issue is. The resolution can be evoked by helping the person exhibit more creative dream ego interaction in the second re-enactment. Encourage the other dream actors to interact differently with the dream ego if necessary. Sometimes they will respond well to the new behaviour on their own.

7. Once the resolution occurs, stop the action, do not linger. Have people sit right where they are and talk about their own feelings of the experience. Do not focus on the dreamer, who needs time

simply to feel the effects rather than become too conscious and interact. Finally the dreamer may want to say a few words. The leader can then objectify briefly what happened in the experience, and take questions and reactions from those who did not participate directly.

8. Encourage the dreamer to write up his or her experience and send you as leader a copy. This brings out the essence and gives them a task to make what has been a deeply emotional experience more conscious. They will feel different and it will have direct effects on their everyday living. Also keep track of similar dreams in the future to see how changes are happening there.

Effects

• As with Dream Re-entry, profound feeling effects can occur because a successful enactment changes an underlying pattern or block in the psyche.

• A sense of devotion and depth of meaning occurs in the group. Let them feel it by not moving too quickly to the next person or talking about the experience too much.

• Life changes are made based on the experience because fundamental patterns in the person have been amplified and at least partially resolved.

THE DREAM ARTS

All art is symbolic expression of the same dynamics reflected in dreams. Painting dream scenes in vivid colours makes their symbolism stand out at a feeling level. Enacting parts of a dream in movement with or without music helps the dreamworker feel the symbolic energy in the body and psyche united. Do not worry about needing to be an artist or dancer. Many people are afraid to do art as adults because of childhood judging experiences. Recognise these memories but move through them by letting go to the creative flow. Your psyche will know better what to do in embodying a dream's energy than your ego will. Let go and let flow. Making a dream's energy part of your felt experience enables you to better actualise the dream's potential in you and your life. Buy an art notebook and some oil pastels or crayons to start. These will give vivid colours and are easy to use.

DREAM INCUBATION

To evoke a dream on a given issue focus before sleep on the issue. Write out how you see the problem and potential and how you might choose. Then create a key question which captures the essence of your issue, write it on paper and put it under your pillow. At dawn wake and write quickly anything which is there in your head, dream or not. Do this for three days if no dream has come the first morning. Then compare the dream with the issue, looking for similarity in imagery, values, choices, possible outcomes. The Dream Source usually will not give an answer but may give a dream which deepens the issue. Not whom should I relate to but how do I relate? is the kind of question the Dream Source best responds to. Also ask yourself, to what question or issue is this dream a response to? Objectifying Dreams, Following the Dream Ego, Dream Researching, and Key Questions are the methods to use to tune into the incubated dream. Then do Dream Tasks, the dreamwork which brings the potential of the incubated dream into actuality. *Do not ask if you will refuse to hear.* Also use this method to help you remember dreams.

RESEARCHING DREAM THEMES

Analysing for theme is when you look at a series of dreams for common symbols, actions, dream ego behaviour, and make comparisons between dreams based on these repeat symbols. *First you categorise the specifics and then you generalise from them.* Generalising means making broad but accurate statements about content. The general organises the specific and makes it meaningful. From the *specific* the *context* emerges. The next stage is to discover the same theme or pattern within yourself and within your life, and then to formulate changes you will make to that theme or pattern based on the insight and work already accomplished with your dreams.

When to use

- When you need insight about a major problem or pattern. Follow your dreams. They know better than you what is going on.

- When undergoing a major review of your life, say in preparation for a birthday or for celebrating the transition into the New Year.

- Use as a form of self-study about yourself, perhaps taking your life in three-month segments and reviewing the dreams for major themes during each of these periods. *We cannot become conscious of who we are without reflection upon who we have been.*

Step by step method

1. For a given period select those dreams which have a common theme in symbol, action, or dream ego activity.
2. Make lists of the actual symbols, actions, dream ego activity, which fall within the theme you are researching. Date the entries.
3. Look for *similarity*, *contrast*, and *progression*.
4. Generalise. Once clear on the content, go from the specific to the general. Use functional statements where appropriate. Create essence statements from your generalisations.
5. Apply the general and essence statements to your personality and life. You may have to do the same research method on an area of your outer life. Once you are clear on your dream life theme and your outer life theme you can make meaningful comparisons.
6. Now formulate changes in attitude and behaviour you would like to make. Choose what is possible now and commit yourself to specific actions you will soon take. Go from the general to the specific.
7. Look for future dreams to symbolise the progress or to challenge you on how you are working with your theme.
8. This method can be done thoroughly or quickly. The quick way is to read each step here and make yourself intuit rapidly whatever comes into consciousness without thinking about it. Whatever approach you take, keep pushing through to the end. The Dream Source is maintaining a record of your life, following, as it must, hundreds of themes. Why not tune in?

Effects

- Through this work the practitioner is able to understand major life areas, and to find the next growth steps in them.
- The method helps you analyse unconscious patterns governing your actions. Gaining such insight allows you to construct tasks for changing these patterns for the better.
- The method allows you to review your life and thus gives you a sense of meaning and direction. We learn who we are, where we are going, and what to do to get there.

GROUP DREAMING

Creating a group dream together enlivens the psyche of each individual in the group. A group dream is produced by the group going together into a meditative state and opening up to the Dream Source. Each person sits in the circle holding hands and meditating, letting go to whatever images will come. As the images arrive they become stimulated by each other and the dream builds. People feel the energy and yet remain grounded and able to assimilate the dynamics evoked. evoked.

DREAMWORK AND THERAPY

A major value of including dreamwork with therapy is that it allows both client and therapist to focus directly on a broader view of the person than either the therapist or client alone can create. Dreamwork is also a specific growth project one does at home, and this adds to the effect of the therapy. *We learn about dreamwork from doing it.* Both therapist and client can use this book to do in-depth dreamwork. The dreams will teach each what they need to know if they make the commitment to the work. Dreamwork can also provide breakthroughs when needed in the therapeutic process as well as mirror projections and counter-projections of client and therapist.

SYMBOL AMPLIFICATION

This method is not needed if doing process dreamwork. Yet it is a quick tool for gaining insight. The Dream Source takes outer images to symbolise dream dynamics. To understand an image or action as symbol in a dream, recall how that symbol functions in the outer. A car functions to take us places and to protect. It symbolises effectiveness and ego control, among other things. By looking at function rather than concept we understand the symbol as a dynamic living energy. Next we look at the symbol within its context in the dream. We look at the specific way the Dream Source is using the general symbol. Then we look at the dream ego's relation to the symbol in the dream. Using the Seven Basic Archetypes model also helps understand how the symbol is functioning in the dream and how it refers to outer life as well. We see which archetype seems dominant and what would be its counterbalancing energy which might resolve the dream situation.

SOURCE IMMERSION

We can relate to source energies through Source Immersion as well as through dreams. It is unnecessary to simply wait for a dream to contact the Dream Source. Think of this method as opening a door inside yourself and letting whatever is there come. *You can have a dream any moment of your life if you can learn how to open whenever you need to.* When in the midst of an issue, close your eyes for a moment, picture the situation as it is, then let spontaneous resolving imagery emerge. This may point to creative action, even if not what your personal ego wanted.

7 · LEVELS OF DREAMWORK

Dreamwork is learned as a skill through commitment and practice. The following levels descriptions will show what can be achieved at various stages of the work. They show that dreamwork can be clearly defined as a practical skill. For evaluating oneself respond in writing or discussion to each of these descriptors, giving your present experience and what you would like to achieve. This is how you start. In six months to a year's time re-evaluate yourself.

LEVEL 1

- Remembering at least one dream a week with sufficient detail to understand some sense of the pattern involved.

- Writing or tape recording dreams regularly.

- Having a positive and open attitude towards one's own dreams.

- Remembering at least four dreams from the past year.

- Remembering at least five major dreams in one's lifetime.

- Being able to listen to someone else's dreams without rationally interpreting them for that person.

- Making the choice to give up rationally interpreting one's own dreams.

- Making definite changes in one's life based on principles and practices revealed in dreamwork.

- Being aware of at least four major themes or issues over the past year which recur in a series of dreams.

Comment: Note that even before one can be considered at Level 1 the dreamworker will have dealt with the following:

- Not remembering dreams at all because one's focus is solely on the outer life.

- Not remembering dreams because one has had a traumatic experience, usually in childhood, regarding one's own unconscious.

- Not remembering and recording dreams because of egocentric attitudes against having experiences in which one's conscious ego is not in control.

- Not remembering and recording dreams because one has not yet chosen to stand up to one's spouse, parents or society regarding the right to develop an inner life.

- Interpreting other people's dreams for them because one has a rational approach to life which is used to try to maintain control of oneself and others.

LEVEL 2

- Remembering at least three to four dreams a week.
- Doing dreamwork with at least one dream a week.
- Sharing dreams and dreamwork with at least one other person on a regular basis.
- The dream ego has shifted from being primarily an observer to being active in at least one remembered dream a week.
- The dreamer is committed to recording all remembered dreams, given time limitations, not just 'good' ones favoured by the ego.
- The dreamer is dealing with at least some adversarial dreams by staying in them through the crisis, or point of greatest fear.
- The dreamer is making shifts from a defensive and victimish personality to one operating from a healing centre in dreams and life.
- The dreamer has gone through a death experience in at least one dream.
- The dreamer has experienced several Great or Resolving dreams during the present time and worked with them to produce life changes.

- Certain major issues or themes appearing in one's dreams have gone through a transformation process regarding both one's life and one's dreams.

- One has received Confirming dreams regarding major shifts in one's consciousness and life.

- One's dream life and dreamwork is developed to the extent that they are the major sources for perspective about oneself and direction in life.

- One follows one's dreams through choice and not identification or interpretation. One actualises one's dreams.

- The dreamworker has developed at a basic level a dreamwork methodology for working with his or her own dreams.

- One has pretty much dealt with the inflationary tendency to extrovert one's dreamwork by showing it off in the world.

- One actively shares dreams and dreamwork with others of like commitment, receiving and giving Dream Tasks and support. This also creates a dream community relatedness.

- One is dealing with projections on to people and situations, thus seeing that outer life is also a dreamlike symbolic experience.

- The dreamwork now includes these basic channels of expression: dream ego work, bringing resolution, healing centre work, choice-making, consciousness, dreambody and other body expression, spiritual perspective and direction, healing traumatic and defensive dynamics, symbolic expression such as in the arts, personality change, relationship with others.

Comment: Level 2 is obviously the basic dreamwork level. Level 1 describes those who are exploring dreamwork for themselves but have not made a full commitment to it as a major practice. Level 2 people will at least actively practise dreamwork for a certain period of their lives, if not all their lives. Both Levels 1 and 2 require some outside support system such as regular attendance at a dream group or working with someone individually. Group work itself aids the process and creates a sense of community or common purpose. You may or may not be ready to begin teaching others. You may have the talent for it, but have you gone through your own transformation enough so you are not acting out of inflation by an archetype? This is a devilish question. Follow it closely in your dreams.

LEVEL 3

- You have been actively involved in your own dreamwork for at least two years. This does not mean simply recording dreams but working with them.

- You have gone through a major transition or transformational process based on your dreamwork and other growth processes.

- You have dealt with the control issue in yourself and in your dreams. You no longer seek to have the dominant say in dream activity or outer relationships.

- You respond to dream challenge by staying present in at least half of your adversarial dreams, dealing with the situation in a variety of ways.

- You are able to deal with adversarial situations in life with the same openness and creativity required in dreams.

- You have achieved a basic congruence between dream life and waking life. What you do creatively in dreams you also do in life.

- You work with all types of dreams from boring dreams to Great dreams, from Adversarial dreams to pleasure dreams.

- You are actively following your dream ego in all the recorded dreams and have changed many of its incongruent attitudes and actions.

- Your dream ego is often in relation to and active in the dream's actions.

- You have a number of dreams which resolve themselves on their own. The others you work with to actively bring resolution to them.

- You are basically non-defensive in your outer life because you have dealt with adversarial and traumatic dreams as they come up and applied the results to life.

- You have an active and in depth dreamwork practice regarding your dreams.

- Your dream life has also become a source of spiritual wisdom and transcendent experience.

- You are having great dreams every so often in which you are active with but not in control of source energies.

- You are much less projected out onto the world and understand the difference between the inner and outer life.

- You are following your intuitive knowing in much that you do.

- You are teaching or sharing with others in an open manner, and according to your talents, dreamwork skills, and other practices.

- Your life is not your own.

Comment: Even beginners will see elements of themselves in all the levels descriptions. We can only describe guidelines. The main thrust here is that dreamwork is a practice which develops and becomes more dynamic the more you do it. Many people will study for a while and experience the basics, thinking they have obtained a sense of the process. And they have. But then the hard work begins through commitment. The dynamism of dreamwork grows the more you practise it. The amazing thing is that its core process, the dream, is always revealing itself to us. For greater reward greater work is required. The work also becomes more fluid the more you practise. Dreamwork is not for everybody, or is it, since we all dream? Could dreamwork be for everyone, even the scared and the lazy, because the dream function is an expression of the self-regulating centre of each and every person's psyche? You have that choice. What you choose is what you become.

LEVEL 4

- The dreamworker has been tested by life and him or herself. Ongoing dreamwork is an integral part of life.

- Major dreams always seem to lead to major life changes.

- Life transitions are accompanied by prospective and confirming dreams.

- Life is not lived through identification with the outer world. One processes outer life like a dream.

- A depth of spiritual energy is available to this person for personal use and universal healing. Synchronistic events may accompany significant acts.

- The personality of the dreamer is as multifaceted and paradoxical as the dreams themselves.

- One is usually skilled and effective in living life to the core.

- Nothing matters because everything matters.

APPENDIX 1

THE MAJOR TYPES OF DREAMS

As you have noticed, sixty-four of the sixty-six dream examples in the book have a dream type classification with a short explanation. It helps in looking at a dream to tell what kind of dream it is, or especially how it functions. This awareness helps us do better dreamwork in applying dreams to life. Be aware that the same dream can have more than one classification. We are not separating chickens from apples! When working with a dream use this list to classify it, and then give your dream its own title.

Amplifying dreams – Dreams may heighten certain life situations or attitudes to make them quite obvious to the dreamer.

Archetypal dreams – The Dream Source may show the dreamer which archetypal energies are most active in her, or a life situation, so they may be made conscious and be dealt with.

Childhood dreams – Contemporary dreams may reflect childhood dynamics needing resolution. Remembered dreams from early childhood almost always show the mythic pattern re-enacted over and over in a person's life journey.

Children's dreams – Children can work with their dreams as effectively as adults, using intuitive processes such as art and story telling.

Compensatory dreams – Dreams will present a viewpoint about an issue which is different or contrary to the dominant ego view.

Confirming or Complementary dreams – When we seem to have made an effective or meaningful choice in life we will often receive a dream which confirms this action.

Ego Issues dreams – Dreams will sometimes present the dream and waking egos with issues of attitude, feeling, and behaviour needing change.

Expressive dreams – We are able to experience in dreams at an imagery and feeling level certain things not possible in outer life.

Great dreams – The Great dream is a dream which contains a major issue of one's life with its possible resolution and new insight felt at a feeling level.

Intuition dreams – Sometimes dreams reveal information about outer people and situations so that we may act consciously to prepare for and resolve them.

Issues dreams – Dreams may present us with inner and outer problems so we may do dreamwork to resolve them.

Lucid dreams – Dreams in which the waking ego and dream ego are merged producing conscious recognition that one is dreaming, often by the ego function taking over the image-making function from the Dream Source.

Nightmare dreams – Dreams which have adversarial elements confronting the dream ego may become nightmares if the waking ego blocks, due to fear, and wakes the dream ego before the resolution to the dream situation can occur.

Predictive dreams – Dreams may alert us to major outer events about to happen.

Prospective dreams – Dreams may show us potentials for new growth and direction in life as well as problems to be dealt with.

Psychic dreams – In Psychic dreams we perceive things intuitively which we would not know otherwise.

Relationship dreams – Some dreams reveal accurately the dynamics of a close relationship and even what to do about them.

Revelatory dreams – Sometimes dreams will reveal new possibilities for action and insight.

Sexual dreams – Dream sex may reflect the archetypal pattern underlying outer life sex, as well as be an experience of unity with another part of ourselves.

Shadow-persona or Skunk dreams – Dreams help us disidentify from our personas by picturing us in shadow behaviour.

Spiritual dreams – Spiritual dreams give us a major perspective about our ego's relation to source energies.

Teaching dreams – Certain dreams will train the waking ego by putting the dream ego through difficult situations in new ways which resolve them and help the person learn new life wisdom.

Unresolved dreams – Unresolved dreams are dreams which present issues in stasis or conflict without resolution.

Waking dreams – Sometimes an inner situation may become so intense, and need resolution so badly, that it breaks into outer life creating scenes loaded with symbolism about the person's life choices.

APPENDIX 2

DEFINITIONS IN DREAMWORK

The following definitions represent the key concepts for practising dreamwork. It is necessary to know these through direct experience.

Acceptance: The choice to open oneself to the way things are.

Actualising dreams: The practice of re-experiencing dreams and the bringing of their content into everyday life.

Amplification: Discovering the meaning of a symbol or other experience through objectifying the inherent characteristics of the symbol or other experience.

Anger: The emotion of repressed feeling. When we do not express but repress we are causing life energy to dam up until it explodes into anger.

Archetype: A cluster of energy and form inherent in existence. A basic pattern of energy expression which manifests as energy and form, as image, as pattern, as functions within the personality, as roles in society, as feelings, and finally as concepts and symbols.

Choice: The directing of energy in one direction and not another. The saying Yes to one thing while saying No to all that would oppose it.

Consciousness: Awareness plus appropriate action. To be truly aware is to act on that awareness.

Destiny: What we do with fate through choice. We might not choose what happens to use but we can choose how we deal with what happens.

Dialogue: A dreamwork method in which you access dynamics in your psyche other than ego and give them a voice.

Dream Ego: The focus of the dreamer's self-identity while in the dream. This may be the dreamer's image or merely a felt presence of awareness without specific form, or even awareness but in another form.

Dream Re-entry: A dreamwork method in which you place yourself in a meditative state and go back into your dream from the waking state in order to re-experience your dream more fully and possibly resolve it.

Dream Source: That centre within the psyche which uses the image-making function of the psyche to create inner experiences of meaning and need for integrative balance when the person is asleep.

Dream: An inner experience in action, feeling, imagery, and sometimes word which is produced by non-ego sources, namely the Dream Source.

Dreamwork: Working with dreams to enhance their content, bring out the meaning they have for the dreamer, and stimulate and create change.

Ego: The personality function which focuses awareness, makes choices, and is the locus of individual identity.

Emotion: An over-riding energy state in the psyche which subverts specific feeling states to its mood.

Feeling: The experience within of either positive (going towards) or negative (withdrawing) energy, which then gets expressed in voice or action.

Feminine: The archetype of openness, flow, and encompassing reality.

God: Non-ego source energy of greater power and wisdom than the ego can of itself create. Other terms: Source, Divinity, Sacred, Dream, Reality.

Image-Making Function: that predisposition to action in the psyche which takes affective energy and translates this into images for processing as dreams, memories and other internal visualisations.

Individuation: A life-long process of becoming conscious about one's own true nature and following that nature rather than collective values and attitudes. Ongoing dreamwork is necessary to discovering and following one's own inner nature.

Inner Experience: Mental and physical states felt and perceived as coming from within and expressed in feeling, imagery, action, and concept.

Interpretation: Asserting what a symbol means based on applying an outside symbol system to an original experience.

Intuition: The direct perception of the potential and the inherent character of a thing or experience.

Journey: The experience of integrating one's inner awareness and development with one's outer awareness and development. Also, a sense of living one's inherent predisposition and purpose in life.

Jungian-Senoi Dreamwork: A comprehensive dreamwork approach combining a full dreamwork methodology with a strong perspective on the nature of the spiritual and psychological journey.

Life Force: The energy, the ability to move matter, within oneself and life.

Masculine: The archetype of focus, direction, and goal orientation.

Meaning: The inherent relations between things.

131

Meditative State: A mental state of inner awareness in which the ego allows inner dynamics to unfold.

Numinous: The energic or evocative aspect of a symbol or sacred experience.

Objectivity: Perceiving the inherent nature of a thing based on perceiving both our own subjective bias and experiencing directly the object of our awareness.

Observing Ego: The individual point of awareness which observes actions and other mental states and has self-identity.

Opposites: Primary energies or archetypes which exist in relation to each other through harmony and opposition.

Pain: The experience of resisting the life force.

Participating Ego: The individual point of awareness with self-identity which also involves itself in an experience and takes action.

Persona: The positive side of the personality made up of self-identity images and attitudes which are considered positive by the individual and possibly the culture within which he or she dwells.

Pleasure: The experience of the life force flowing freely through one.

Psyche: The totality of the inner world of a person which has the integrative centre of the Self, the dynamics of the unconscious, the ego, the persona, the shadow, and other dynamics such as the parent-child complexes and archetypal manifestations.

Reality: That which *is* by force of being. The effect of energy and matter which over-rides the subjective symbol systems of the individual.

Religion: A collective belief and practice occurring in groups of people.

Resistance: The attempt by the ego and other parts of the psyche to remain within known patterns and attitudes in the face of new growth being evoked.

Resolution: The art of evoking a change in a conflictual pattern or situation which then allows any of its dynamics to be harmonised or destroyed.

Self: Capitalised, the Self is the integrative centre within the personality. It utilises the archetype of centre in the universe itself, and so may also refer to the centre which is in all things.

Sex: The experiencing of the life force through the archetypal experience of unity.

Shadow: That side of the personality which is hidden from the persona, the conscious side the ego is identified with.

Soul: A word for referring to the relationship between the ego and the centre of the psyche and of life. The soul is the personal aspect of the Self.

Source: Another term for the Self but indicating source energies wherever they are inner and outer. Source energies are those potentials which offer renewal, meaning, transformation, as a new life if the ego would but give up control and serve and actualize these source energies.

Spiritual: The experience of source energies other than ego which happen to the individual. Spiritual experience happens only to individuals, even if generated in a group, is direct, and not based on collective belief and practice.

Subjective: The inner mental processes which colour our perceptions of what is outside us.

Suffering: The tension between a person's present physical and emotional state and the new state demanded by forces greater than ego.

Symbol: A cluster of images and energy which evokes many levels of meaning.

Symbol Immersion: A meditative state technique for experiencing images and actions at an inner level.

Symbol System: A loosely organised conglomeration of images, attitudes, and concepts which the individual and societies use as the basis for organising their behaviour and making choices. No symbol system is reality itself but only an approximation of what the perceivers assert reality is like.

Synchronicity: Meaningful coincidence. The convergence of separately happening events and dynamics, inner and outer, which together produce a meaningful pattern involving the specific consciousness of a person.

Transformation: Change which changes the totality of an individual, group, or situation towards greater meaning, wholeness and life.

Truth: That which is real by direct knowing, either through experience or through intuition. The direct perceiving of core essences behind manifestations of the concrete.

Unconscious: A term used for that part of the psyche which we do not know consciously. The Unconscious is only one part of the total psyche.

Wholeness: An on-going process of making conscious and including all parts of oneself, including the shadow side, within a harmonizing and differentiating whole.

APPENDIX 3

WHERE TO GO IF YOU WANT TO GO FURTHER.

For those interested in working further with dreams in this approach please contact The Dream Cards Institute, 115, 1592 Union Street, San Francisco, California 94123, USA.

Other books by the author which will be of great interest to the reader are: *The Dreamwork Manual*, a fully comprehensive handbook for working with dreams, (Journey Press); *Transforming Childhood*, a unique handbook for personal growth, (Element Books) and *The Practice of Personal Transformation*, a revolutionary approach to conscious change, (Journey Press).

The author has also developed *The Dream Cards*, (Simon & Schuster). A beautifully illustrated set of cards using synchronicity and analysis to work with dreams.

For writing to the author, or obtaining information about his books and tapes, contact the publishers or the following address:
Journey Press – Publisher's Services
P.O.Box 2510
Novato, CA94948
USA

INDEX